KEEP
YOUR EYE ON THE
PRIZE

*A Story of Determination,
Diligence, and Perseverance*

Kenneth L. Holmes

Keep Your Eye on the Prize
Copyright Kenneth L. Holmes

ISBN: 978-1-7352724-5-0
Printed in the United States of America

Cover and book design: Abraham Obafemi Emmanuel
Editor: Kathleen Tracy
Cover illustration: Lucas Henrique da Gama

To my dear mother, who I'm sure is an angel in heaven still looking after me.

ACKNOWLEDGMENTS

I would like to thank Darlene Roberto, who as superintendent of schools saw in me what others did not. I am forever grateful for her having the faith in me and going to bat for me, which led me to being named principal of Abraham Clark High School from 1996 to 2001.

I would also like to acknowledge Jean Burgdorff, former owner of Burgdorff Realtors, who was kind enough to give me a personal loan when she didn't even know me, which marked the beginning of my financial success. I am forever thankful and will never forget her caring and compassion towards me.

CONTENTS

PREFACE

Since I was very young, I have always felt uneasy labeling people White, Black, Asian, East Indian, American Indian, Hispanic, and Hawaiian, etc. But things are getting so bad today with all the division that using the words Black and White almost seems like a necessity. That hits me in the pit of my stomach.

Okay, people do come from different parts of the world, but why do we have to be identified by where we come from or by our color? We're all here in the land of *Give me your tired, your poor, and your huddled masses yearning to breathe free*. What happened to that? Is it all a lie? I pray that my great-granddaughter, who just turned one while writing this book, will get to see the above words come true in her lifetime.

I don't know how many of you have seen the original *Star Wars* film, but the space bar scene, where humans, creatures, and aliens in all manner of colors and shapes share drinks and couldn't care less about what each other looked like, it says it all. In my lifetime I have been called Negro, colored, Afro American, Black, and the N-word on an ongoing basis. It would be a wonderful world if I could be just Ken.

I was never a social media fan. I prefer keeping my personal business to myself. I prefer texts or WhatsApp. I guess I'm old school. But I had wanted to locate a few friends and was finally talked into joining Facebook. I was most interested in finding a former exchange student of mine from Germany. And thirty years or so after I taught him, we reconnected. It turned out he'd been looking for me too. He posted about our reunion on Facebook, which caused an avalanche of former students, coworkers, and friends asking to be Facebook friends. After I friended some people, it caused a chain reaction of even more former students and friends making friend requests.

Some posts from former students made me smile, and others were like pulling a scab off an old wound. Those four years of Trump brought back old memories of BS I'd gone through all my life. Then reading the remarks from some of my former students and friends on top of that really upset me. I remember in the late fifties and sixties watching demonstrations, burnings, and looting, with Black people getting attacked by fire hoses, nightsticks, and dogs.

As far as the burning and looting, it sickened me in the past, and it sickens me now. The people who do such things should be caught and put in jail regardless of whether they are poor Blacks, Browns, or Whites. We also have White supremacist implants burning, looting, and defacing property to weaken the message of the peaceful protestors. Some media and politicians use that deception to try and distort the big picture.

It sickens me to see Black men get murdered on national TV and some police still get away with it. I am sure Black men were being murdered by White policemen on a daily basis in the past, but without all of today's social media, who would know? My grandfather told stories of Black men getting hanged by the Ku Klux Klan (KKK) for even just looking at a White woman, and there wasn't any use of calling the police because most of the time, the chief of police was involved in the hanging. I have nothing against the police in general because I have friends who are good policemen.

Racial profiling isn't anything new to me, especially since I often drove a high-end vehicle like a Rolls Royce, Mercedes, or Hummer. I can't count the times police have stopped me for no apparent reason. Sometimes they'd use the phony excuse that I was crossing the center line, had taillights out, or was speeding. A few times the officer would outright ask me whose car it was and how I could afford it—of course, some of my neighbors in West Virginia and New Jersey asked the same thing. Some White people believe that Black people aren't supposed to have what they have or more than what they have. I don't know if it's a mentality carried over from the days of slavery or simple, outright jealousy, but I can relate in a different way.

Imagine that you own a hunting dog and a workhorse. You give them a place to sleep out back in the barn and feed them every day. They are both a necessity in your daily life. You hunt game to eat with the dog and use the horse for transportation and plowing the fields. But now you have to free these animals, and they'll be given the same rights and opportunities that you have. The dog and the horse are now getting houses, cars, and everything else that is just as good or better than what you have. How would you feel?

I admit that I would be upset as a Black man with this new way of life but would eventually get over it. I wouldn't pass on hate to my children, causing them to give hate to their children. The buck has to stop somewhere.

Speaking of animals, I remember times growing up when some White people would say: *I'm not prejudiced; I've had Black people at my house for dinner, and I let them eat off my plates, spoons, and forks.*

Wow, that made me feel good.

It also hurt when White former students and friends—who called themselves friends of mine, who called themselves friends of other Blacks, Asian, Muslim, and Brown people—excused all of Trump's racial comments, sophomoric behavior, despicable comments about people in general, corruption, draft-dodging, and knocking the military and them claimed that he only lost because the election was rigged.

It's like they were brainwashed. Trump himself said, "If you keep repeating something [a lie] long enough, people will believe you."

I gave a pass to those friends that voted for him the first time because they went for all the lies that he told. I believed they thought he was going to help them pay fewer taxes. I heard some people say they voted for him because he was against abortion. Do you mean to tell me that you looked past all the hate and corruption because of one policy that he was more than likely lying about anyway?

I read comments like *There is no such thing as White privilege because everyone is equal no matter your color; you have to work hard to get ahead. There isn't any systemic racism in this country.*

Yes, working hard to get ahead is so true because I'm a product of that. I wouldn't have been successful if it weren't for some White people who weren't afraid to live up to or admit their White privilege by sticking their necks out to lend a helping hand. Yes, just turn on your televisions and see who's out there demonstrating for Black Lives Matter—millions of White people living up to the fact that they have White privilege. But admitting White privilege doesn't mean you're obligated to give away some of what you have. Not anyone is going to take anything from you. All people want is equal opportunity.

Many White people get offended when they hear the phrase Black Lives Matter, and they say that White lives matter too. The whole world already knew for centuries that White lives matter, so when I hear that rebuttal to Black Lives Matter, I think they're saying: *To hell with Black, Asian, and Brown people.* Or is it possible they just don't know what's really happening around them? Maybe the phrase should be Black Lives Matter Too. How would the naysayers respond to that?

White people, including White clergy, marched for Black Lives Matter back in the '50s and '60s, risking their lives. Some lost their lives for the cause. The slogan Black Lives Matter may be fairly new, but it's been innate in all Black people since the beginning of time. Many White people have admitted their White privilege by assisting Black people in their struggle more than a hundred years before the '50s and '60s, hence the Underground Railroad, Abraham Lincoln, and abolitionist John Brown, to name a few events and people that believed Black Lives Matter.

In my opinion, when you're White and not afraid to admit that

Black Lives Matter publicly, you are admitting your White privilege. Earlier I mentioned that White people helped me throughout my life, and it isn't putting them on a pedestal but highlighting those who admit their White privilege.

Not one of the hundreds or thousands of my former students, personal friends, peers, or coworkers has any idea of my life's struggles because I never mentioned it to any of them. So most people know me as Mr. Holmes, a happy-go-lucky person, a guy who gave them a little job while in or out of high school, a teacher who cared about students, a nice guy that showed compassion, a guy who gave them good advice, a guy that dressed nice, and had nice cars and homes.

Throughout life I've been told that I was different by childhood friends, adult friends, and acquaintances. I would sometimes ask what they meant just to put them on the spot. Most of the time I'd get a distorted answer and would let them off the hook by changing the subject.

There would be times, though, when I'd get the answer I already knew and didn't really want to hear: *You don't rob and steal, you dress differently, and you talk White.* With these hard cases, I had to tell them they needed to get out in the real world more and not to compare me with what they saw on the news and in movies. Those slaps in my face would sometimes be the end of whatever friendship we had.

I also had some Black students say that I talked White—usually students I was disciplining or their disgruntled and irate parents. Those remarks were meant to infer I thought I was above them by the way I talked. Needless to say this particular topic led to a whole new topic of geography, phonetics, and assimilation.

I'm guessing that some White people looked at me as a White man in a Black body. For the first twenty years of my life, I was a Black person who was only exposed to White people because my father had relocated the family to an entirely White town. While living in that environment, I never thought that I was better than other Black people—or any other nationality or race. I was often reminded by some White people that I was just the N-word. I truly believe that a Black person living in that environment in the fifties and sixties for the first twenty years of their life could be brainwashed to believe that they didn't count as an equal human being. You never saw any Black achievement in schoolbooks, just depictions of Black children and adults with big lips, barefoot, and straw hats.

Stories from my father and grandfather's life experiences would offset the obfuscation in the schoolbooks. But it wasn't until I attended college—at a school that practiced Jim Crow segregation my first two years—that I learned about American history from a professor who dared to teach the truth. I couldn't wait to hear his next lecture and would get to his classroom fifteen minutes early.

Some former students who weren't involved with all that negative political rhetoric on Facebook gave me their phone numbers to call them if I wished and vice versa. They remembered going camping on my property, going skiing, fun in gym classes, working in my office, and the house I built on my property. Some asked if I still lived there.

No, that town wasn't all it was trumped up to be.

How so?

I told them about one particular racial event that happened to me in 2000. Two former students said they couldn't believe that kind of behavior was still happening. I thought: *My God, how they could possibly think that racism wasn't still around.* Does that mean they have no idea what's going on all around them right now, or is it because they wanted to make me feel better without realizing what they were saying? Were they trying to placate me? Or was it because it wasn't of any concern of theirs back then and of no concern of theirs now?

Those comments on Facebook and comments to me personally prompted me to write this book about my life. I hope all my former students, coworkers, peers, friends, people in general, and young people of all races—especially young people of color—will know my story and see how perseverance and diligence pay off in the end. My ten siblings and I went through adversity all our lives, and none of us had to depend on government assistance. Four of us would become millionaires. Hopefully, people who have privilege will see the world that we live in for what it really is—unless they are outright hatters and refuse to see it.

INTRODUCTION

My grandfather Genius Holmes was born in Hillsborough, Georgia, the son of slaves Sarah Whiting and Burial Holmes, my great-grandparents. And he was a boy slave. Even though slavery officially ended the year he was born, 1863, some places in the South alleged they didn't find out about the Emancipation Proclamation until two or more years later, communication being what it was back then. I'm guessing that some slave owners knew it but ignored the law.

Genius married Camilla Vincent, and they had nine children. While living in the South, he owned and managed a large farm and also owned a confectionary store. He bought a farm after Reconstruction. In addition to his business and farming skills, this strong, proud man had musical talents and played in a family band with four other brothers, performing at church functions, dances, and other occasions in several surrounding towns. He later sold his farm and moved to a little town in Ohio called Rayland, where he worked in the steel industry as a custodian. He was also a Freemason.

My grandfather while living in Hillsborough, GA, on his farm

He would tell stories about being the only Black living in town and how he could see burning crosses a couple of miles away on a hillside. He came all the way to Ohio just to see more crosses burn. But he refused to be intimidated, saying that he would die before he'd be frightened away. He'd seen enough of that kind of behavior all of his life.

My father, Burial Holmes, was born in Hillsboro, Georgia in 1902, and left the South to get away from farming for his father, sharecropping, and Jim Crow—it wasn't unusual for him to see Black folks hanging from a tree. Once my father saved enough money, he moved to Martins Ferry, Ohio, a town with very few Black people. But that's where he met and married my mother, Dorothy, a hometown girl fifteen years his junior. He got a job at a coal mine that enabled him to save money and send for some of his siblings.

I was originally conceived in 1942, but that baby died of pneumonia a few months later. They conceived again, and on March 26, 1943, there I was again—déjà vu. My parents were churning out a child just about every year, eleven in total—me twice and nine more—some of us born at home and some in the hospital.

It's just my luck that I landed on the same poor ass family twice.

After child number five (me), my dad moved us to Rayland and purchased a home that had previously belonged to his brother Leonard who had moved to Detroit. This mostly White town now had three Black families—all on my father's side—living a stone's throw away from each other: our grandparents, Uncle John and his family, and us.

Later in life my siblings and I were all grateful that our dad had moved us out of Martins Ferry because while there, we lived across the tracks and down by the river in a poverty-stricken area where Black folks were forced to live. My father wanted better for us, and that's why we ended up in blue-collar Rayland, where you either worked in the steel mill or the coal mine. Even though it was just a few miles away, it was a different world for us.

My dad said, "I moved you kids to Rayland to do whatever the White kids do."

I interpreted that to mean he was giving us some adults to aspire to in our new town—grocery store owners, nurses, businessmen, teachers, a couple of lawyers—in contrast to Martins Ferry. I remember going there later in life and observing men standing on the corner, drinking wine. The main entertainment was a couple of juke joints where you could dance and drink. There were a couple of stores in the area: a secondhand store owned by a guy name chicken Mike, who got his nickname by selling live chickens, and a corner liquor store. No, there was not much there for raising children.

LIFE GROWING UP

Uncle John worked in the mill as a janitor and was promoted to driving a dump truck on the mill premises. Grandfather also worked in the mill as a janitor. Skilled labor jobs in those days were only for Whites. I never knew much about my dad's other brothers because they lived in big cities far away. We'd only see them once a year when they dropped by, bragging about how much they had compared to us. I'm guessing it was to make my mother feel bad for all the kids she had; they thought small enough to assume our mother would never leave Rayland.

Uncle John lived up the alley a couple of hundred yards away. He used to cut my brothers' and my hair for a quarter, which my dad didn't pay most of the time. Uncle John had one child named Johnny Jr., who was much older than me and most of my siblings. He was a high school football star that played halfback. I never saw him play, but I heard his name spoken plenty when I was in elementary school.

Uncle John gave Johnny everything. He had his own apartment, which was an unattached garage converted into living quarters. He had a motorbike, movie projector, and keys to his dad's car. Cousin Johnny had it all but didn't go too far in life. Deep down inside I wanted the fame he enjoyed. Uncle John's wife, Geneva, was a nice, quiet lady who treated us nicely when we came for haircuts. Her brother was Sad Sam Jones, a major league baseball pitcher with the San Francisco Giants after the color barrier was broken.

I wanted his fame too, so I practiced and practiced and became one of the best pitchers in little league, pony league, and high school. I was the

I am standing between my lifelong friends Regis Woods and Jim Beck.

starting pitcher in the all-star games in both little league and pony league. I had what you would call a roundhouse curve ball. Batters would fall down backward to get out of the way of the ball, but it would end up going over the plate for a strike. My coaches didn't know any better and would have me pitch sometimes twice a week.

In high school I received letters from the Cleveland Indians and the Pittsburgh Pirates—two of my teachers were scouts for those teams—and I figured that would be my ticket out of poverty. But I threw my arm out in junior year and couldn't hide the pain. Man, if they'd only had Tommy John surgery in those days. But I figured I still had football to save me.

Going back to Sad Sam Jones, I remember him visiting Aunt Geneva when I was probably in the tenth grade. While in town he stopped in at Dad's club one Friday night, the busiest night. The place was packed, and many people were asking him for autographs.

I was helping with the bartending, and Sad Sam pulled me to the side and slipped me enough money for four drinks, paying in advance. He didn't want to buy anyone drinks and told me to sneak the drinks to him when he winked at me. I was so disappointed, not because I expected him to set the house up or even buy one drink for someone; I couldn't believe that someone of his stature would be so cheap. Go figure.

Dad was lucky because he landed a job in a large coal mine, eventually earning $21 a day, which was damn good money in those days—more than $200 in today's money. My dad became friends with some of his White coworkers, visited their homes and farms, and decided that was the way he wanted his kids to live. As an uneducated man—he said he finished third grade, but none of us kids believed him—he learned how to speak Greek from socializing with Greek coworkers.

Our family consisted of four boys and six girls: in order it was Donna, Clara, Burial Jr. who we called Bo, Joann, me, Robert, Dorothy, Sandra, and the twins Geraldine and Gerald, who showed up out of nowhere several years after Sandra. We had no idea that our mother was pregnant because she was a heavyset woman and didn't show. I have to admit it was embarrassing to most of us.

My brother Burial was named after my dad. I guess my grandparents didn't know any better by naming him Burial. My brother would change his name from Burial to Buril while in high school.

I remember when my sister Dorothy was born. A little man went into our mother's bedroom with a black leather bag, and minutes later you could hear a baby crying. I asked my dad where that baby came from; he said the doctor had brought her in his bag, and for years I believed that was where we came from. Sex education from your parents was a no-no in my family.

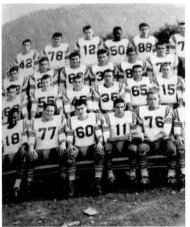

Part of my high school football team: me (#18) as a senior and my brother Bob (#50) as a freshman.

Three of us boys played football, basketball, and baseball. My dad never attended one sporting event except for one college football game, Purdue vs. Ohio State. My brother Bob was co-captain for Purdue, which went to the Rose Bowl that year and played against O. J. Simpson's University of Southern California. I was in Vietnam at that time.

Our dad also never saw any of our report cards, nor did he come to our school for open house or for graduations. He always preached that he didn't ever want to come to schools because of trouble. He would beat you if you stayed home to skip class, but you could stay home to work for him. I remember one time I stayed home because I had no clean underwear and socks. At the time I only had one good pair of each. You had to wash them by hand at night and either put them over the heater grate on the floor or hang them on the open oven door. For some reason, I forgot to wash them and went to bed. I slept in old underwear that had holes in them.

I didn't expect him home so early, and he caught me. He beat me, threw me in the car, and drove me to school. I refused to get out of the car, which was parked a few yards from the front door. He dragged me out with no socks on and beat me all the way to the front door. It was my luck that classes were changing, and some of my football teammates were cheering him on.

It was mortifying going to football practice with fifty other guys and having to get undressed while not wearing any underwear or wearing underwear with holes in them. It was a feat to pull that off without anyone seeing you—and enough to make the average guy quit school.

DETERMINATION

Our dad was a hardworking man and a hustler. He worked me and my brother Bo so hard through the years that we thought he was crazy, until finding out differently when he was in his coffin. My dad died when he was eighty-seven from black lung, caused by long-term exposure to coal dust. I'd see him grimacing all the time, but he'd never tell anyone what was physically bothering him. Some of his old buddies who still lived in the South came to Ohio for his funeral. At the viewing they all lined up in front of his coffin, speaking quietly to one another and shaking their heads. Bo and I went up to find out what they were talking about.

They said that Dad was the hardest working man they'd ever seen. When younger, they had all worked together sharecropping, in the field from six in the morning until daylight ran out. They said our dad would send them back to the house to put their mules in the barn, but he'd stay in the field behind those mules, plowing in the moonlight until midnight or later. They said you could still hear him yelling and whistling at the mules.

Bo, Robert, Geraldine, and I paid for his funeral. We always said our father left us nothing but a funeral bill. He had the best health insurance in the world but never used it for himself or his family. The reason being he didn't know how to use it and was afraid it would cost him money.

Just about all of us kids could have benefitted from seeing the doctor or going to the hospital at some point growing up, but no such thing. When Bo hurt his ankle really badly in high school, he had to pay my father to drive him to the doctor's office. I got the same treatment. I had an abscessed tooth for days before my dad drove me to the dentist, who I had to pay myself. He was an old-school, outdated dentist who had the shakes, probably Parkinson's disease. He opted to pull the molar, and in the process his pulling device slipped and chipped an upper tooth. No comment from my father.

There were plenty of times my poor mother should have seen a doctor. In her late fifties or early sixties she developed glaucoma. Again, she was only able to see an old doctor I'm positive didn't keep up to date on the latest ophthalmology treatments. Some of my siblings and I tried to get her to a modern ophthalmologist, but she was old-fashioned in her ways and resisted, then went blind for the last twenty years or so of her life. Most of us had left the nest by the time our mother discovered that my father had good health insurance.

When I was ten and Bo was about fourteen, my dad leased two large plots of land the size of football fields for farming. We called them the gardens. All gardening was done with a push plow and hoes. My brother and I would work in those fields from sunup to sundown without stopping for breakfast or lunch. We did have a jug of water though. When I see what people call gardens today, I have to laugh. We grew every vegetable you can imagine, and what didn't go in a canning jar, we would sell. Our basement walls were lined with shelves of canned goods. And we had a vegetable stand out in front of the house, which was near two highways.

In my family if you were big enough to walk, you were big enough to go blackberry picking. My father would entice us with two fresh glazed doughnuts each. Then he would pile us into the pickup, including my mother, to go blackberry picking from 7:00 a.m. until late in the evening. We did this several times during the summer, gathering washtubs full of fruit.

A schoolmate's father was an apple farmer who let my siblings and me pick all the apples we wanted, but we were on our own, with no transport from the old man. So we'd push wheelbarrows and wagons at least five miles to the orchard. We'd leave the house at dawn and arrive home late in the evening with hundreds of pounds of apples. We went on this crusade twice a year.

We also had our own pear, purple plum, and peach trees for canning preserves and jelly, huge trees that draped with fruit every year. Then one afternoon our dad came home and cut all three down. We still don't know to this day why he would take food out of our mouths. I've wondered if some farmer had told him how to prune, and he got it very wrong and ended up cutting the trees completely down, or if his coworkers had played a joke on him by saying the trees would come back bigger and better if he cut them down. I am betting on the latter. My father knew how to count money and how to make money but couldn't hang onto it.

Until I was eight or nine, our father was an all-American dad—he was home every day after work, always working around the house and making improvements. The house was nicely painted, had flower beds, manicured grass, and a white picket fence. He'd buy us school clothes—your work clothes were last year's school clothes—and Santa Claus was very good to us. We got bikes, Radio Flyer wagons, sleds, dolls, electric trains, boxing gloves, basketballs, mitts, etc. Sometimes he would even play catch with me with a baseball.

But after my sister Dorothy was born, he abruptly went into complete quit mode. He stayed out all night, stopped buying food, and you could kiss Santa goodbye. I guess he had a method to all his madness with those fields of vegetables and fruits for canning. If it weren't for my three older sisters, things would have been a lot worse. Even though they were still in high school, they had part-time jobs: cleaning houses, working at a hotel in Wheeling, West Virginia, and working in a five-and-dime store. It wasn't much money, but it would buy their clothes and help Mother put some food on the table, especially for Christmas,

Thanksgiving, and Easter.

But toys for Christmas were over. Our sisters would buy us boys some shirts, pants, and underwear. There were no Christmas trees either. On one Christmas Eve, Bo took me to the woods to cut down a little tree because it was bare for the winter and had plenty of branches. We took it into our basement, nailed a flat wooden stand to the bottom, and spray painted it silver. Then we took it upstairs and decorated it as our Christmas tree.

My dad didn't buy many groceries except for occasionally bringing home a fifty-pound can of lard, fifty pounds of flour, a big slab of salt pork, or condiments. We also had about two hundred chickens, mainly for eggs, which we weren't allowed to eat; he'd take them to work and sell them to his coworkers. We couldn't steal any eggs because my dad knew how many eggs were laid daily. The only way we would get a few eggs without him knowing was when hens sometimes flew the coop and went into the woods to lay their eggs. Those eggs wouldn't be part of the count. So we could sometimes get pancakes, egg salad, and homemade cake.

Speaking of sweets, they were a rarity in our household. Pies, cakes, and store-bought bread weren't on the menu until the holidays. All the fruit we canned were used for desserts on holidays, and most of it would be used for our once-a-day meals: apple stew with homemade biscuits, blackberry stew with biscuits, pear preserves, peach preserves, baked sweet potatoes, etc.

Dad once made a deal with the Wonder Bread delivery man to drop off twelve loaves of day-old store bread at our house every other week for ten cents a loaf. My mother would keep it in the basement freezer and ration it out over the next two weeks. But the bread delivery didn't last very long because after the first time, our dad didn't pay him. That Wonder Bread man kept bringing the bread quite a few times despite not getting paid. I think he felt sorry for the little house full of kids.

The basement freezer was also where the old hens that couldn't lay eggs were stored. Mother would roast a couple on holidays and sometimes on Sundays. My dad would put us in an assembly line when slaughtering the old hens and roosters. He would ring their necks, hand them to me and two of my sisters to dip in a tub of boiling hot water and pluck the feathers. Then we passed them to two other sisters to gut and rinse. The last stop was with my mother, who would cut up and bag them.

Bo and I alternated going into the corn crib—rain or shine, summer and freezing winter—and shell a water bucket full of corn by hand, even on school days, which meant getting up at 6:00 a.m. Sometimes my thumbs would bleed from plucking the corn off the cob. Bo always came through with an easier way to do things. He went to the secondhand store and bought a grinder, then ground the cob and all. The chickens loved it and got fatter, my dad loved it, and it was a big burden off of us.

Our mother was more or less in charge of keeping the chickens. I'd go to the post office with her to pick up crates of peeps—so-called because of the noise baby chicks made—that she ordered from a Sears and Roebuck catalog. Then we'd take them home in a wagon. She checked on them daily, and if any of them looked ill, she'd have me pick them up so she could medicate them and separate them from the others until they were healthy.

I hate to admit it, but I was afraid to death of picking up the soft, little creatures. Fortunately, every time she needed my assistance, one of my friends was always around who couldn't wait to handle the little chicks. One day there was no friend around to pick up the chicks. My mother gave me the order to go in and pick up the chicks, and I refused. My face was pressed against the closely webbed wire and glass window as I looked into the coop. My mother gave the back of my head a hard push, causing my face to get engulfed by the wire and breaking the glass behind it. I wasn't cut by the glass, but my face was throbbing and from the wire cutting into my face, causing it to look like a waffle for quite some time. The moral of the story: always do what your mother tells you.

Some years later my friend Clyde who was four years older and a bad influence, would sometimes talk me into stealing a chicken. We'd wait until dark and then sneak into a chicken coop. He taught me that the easiest way to steal a chicken was with a flashlight. When you shine the light in their eyes, they freeze, then you can pick them up with very little squawking.

We had to do the deed before 10:00 p.m. because that's about the time Bo would lock the coops up. We didn't want him to catch us because he might tell the old man, and that would have been the end of my life. And yes, there were a couple of times we were locked in without my brother knowing it. But it was no problem because the "lock" was a swiveling piece of wood with a nail in the middle. I'd trade the stolen chickens with Clyde's mother for a box of Jell-O instant pudding. Shame on her.

In my early teens, before I had my driver's license, we'd load my dad's pickup with produce, then I'd drive my younger siblings around so they could go door-to-door trying to sell it. My job was to weigh, bag, make change, and bag the money. We'd leave the house early in the morning and return in the evening with an empty truck and a bag full of money. Despite the work we did, our dad wouldn't give us one red penny. Ever. We wanted to see our dad prosper, but it would've been nice to get a dime or so once in a while to buy a soda or ice cream.

My father also collected and sold scrap iron and hauled coal for the neighbors. But he never bought coal for our use. We had to scrounge for it to warm our own house. Bo, my older sisters, my dad, and I would go to the slate dump and pick the coal out of the slate until our homemade trailer was full.

Late one evening after picking coal, we were hauling the bulky trailer back with my dad's 1948 Chevy. We were crossing some railroad tracks, and that old car decided to stall right in the middle of the tracks. An oncoming train was coming, blowing its whistle, the huge head lamp getting closer. All of us pushed and pushed with little ground gained. As the train was closing in on us, we seemed to collectively get a shot of adrenaline. With that extra strength, we moved the car and trailer just before the train went flying by.

Bo and I would abscond with a little coal at times. The train cars from the mine were piled high with coal, and the cars seemed to stretch for miles. From our house the tracks where the trains were parked overnight were within walking distance, so we'd go there late at night, throw lots of coal into the weeds, then come back the following day to retrieve it after the cars were pulled away.

The July after our near train wreck, Dad took Robert and me blackberry picking in that same ragged, exhaust-leaking, 1948 Chevy. On the way home my brother and I were in the back seat on our knees, looking out of the rear window. The next thing I remembered was waking up to a horn blaring. My father had passed out, and his body was pressed up against the horn. Robert was also passed out.

We were midway down a steep cliff. I woke up my dad and brother, and we slowly got out of the car. A small tree lodged under the rear right fender was all that was keeping the car from crashing down the remainder of the cliff headfirst into a deep creek below. The leaky muffler was emitting carbon monoxide. Thank God that the motor had stopped running, or we could have all died.

When I was around twelve, Dad would hire my brother and me out to paint houses. It could take several days to finish. Bo would get $50 and me $25, which he would tell us not to spend, to save it. We had no idea how much our dad was paid, but that same night he would come home and borrow our earnings, and we'd never see that money again.

Some of my dad's coworker's houses had crawl spaces for basements, and he would hire us out to dig those basements by hand. When finished, you could walk under the entire house, which were mostly framed, one-story houses. Again, not one red cent was passed our way. Mind you, these jobs and all the aforementioned jobs didn't come with breakfast or lunch.

Well, one couple we were digging a basement for decided to feed us about 2:00 p.m. There were about ten green peas, one piece of Canadian bacon, three or four slices of fried potatoes, a piece of bread, and a glass of ice water. We were very happy to get the food, but it was only a tease. It just so happened that the mother-in-law lived next door and decided to visit just as we started to eat. When she saw our portions of food, she went ballistic on the couple and told us to come next door to get a real meal. We did. It was a feast with a big jelly roll for dessert. We never mentioned that they hadn't offered us food or even water the prior six days; we drank from the water hose on the side of the house when thirsty. I'm guessing that the measly meal the couple offered was our reward since we were finishing up their job that afternoon.

Food always seemed scarce. My siblings and I very rarely got breakfast or lunch on school days or weekends. My brothers and I went without eating all day and then played after-school sports and were usually the best on the teams. We all recall staggering and being lightheaded on the basketball court and the football field. You only got one meal after you arrived home and did your chores. I don't know how we studied and played sports without proper nourishment.

In elementary school there was a ten-minute break every day at 10:00 a.m. to drink some milk, chocolate or plain. But it cost seven cents a week. I never got my hands on those seven cents, so I had to sit and watch the rest of the class drink their milk, which was embarrassing. My dad did not care about the milk break or whether or not I was embarrassed—or hungry. My teachers would sometimes pay for my milk out of sympathy.

When I was in first grade, I had a little Cocker Spaniel that would follow me to school every day. He'd sit at the front entrance and wait. He would also play with children during recess. Then he'd walk home with me. I was allowed to walk home for lunch since we lived nearby, and my mother would try to put something in my stomach, most of the time a bowl of oatmeal. I learned to love oatmeal while in elementary school since there was no other food to offset it. For dinner, no matter what it was my mother had prepared, she had to make me oatmeal.

One day walking home for lunch, I crossed the main street thinking that my dog was right behind me. When I turned to look for him, he was chasing a butterfly right into traffic and was hit by a car and killed instantly.

The driver stopped, rolled his window down, and said, "Keep your damn dog off the street, nigger," and drove off.

My dog's insides were pouring out of him, and they looked just like oatmeal. I picked him up and ran all the way home, hugging him and crying, hoping my mother could bring him back. His insides were smeared all over my hands, face, and clothes. My mother consoled me and helped me bury him. She also let me stay home for the remainder of the day since it was Friday. I haven't eaten oatmeal since that day, and if I saw my baby brothers and sisters eating oatmeal, I would leave the room. I'm okay about it now, but seeing oatmeal still reminds me of that day.

In second grade our teacher would have us read the story, *Jack and the Beanstalk*, about the boy who traded his family's cow for magic beans that led him to a pot of gold. I would be so hungry at times that I imagined Jack's cow being butchered, cut up, and put into a pot with the beans to eat. A nice homemade biscuit would have gone nicely with the beans since that dish was one of our main staples but without the cow (beef).

Lunchtime in high school was the worst. You could buy your lunch at the cafeteria and every day at about 10:30 a.m. I could smell the food.

But I had no money to eat lunch. The school was walking distance to home, but there would only be enough time to touch our gate, turn around, and walk back. The school had an open lunch, so the athletes would go to the football field and sit on the bleachers to eat their lunches, even in the winter. I would be out there with them while they had heavy winter coats, and I would be wearing a jacket and shoes with cardboard on the inside to cover the holes in the sole. The snow and slush would seep through the bottom of my shoes, soaking my socks, which also had holes.

The White guys would have fruit, cake, pie, cookies, and a sandwich or two in their lunches. Every day I'd sit there and say I wasn't hungry. They would sometimes throw away their thick, meat sandwiches since they'd had a big breakfast. I weakened once and accepted their offer of sandwiches.

The following day when one of the guys asked if anyone wanted a sandwich, Ernie Johnson said, "Give it to Kenny; he'll eat it."

My pride was so hurt—that we had no food in the house, plus it was nobody else's business that I was hungry—that I never showed up there again except for football practice. I would walk home and touch my gate every day, then turn around. My mother had no idea.

With very little nutrition and your father making a slave out of you and constantly saying to quit school made it excruciating to endure. My sisters were a little better off with the food situation. They rarely got to eat breakfast, but most of the time they would get to eat lunch. All through elementary school and high school, my sisters were friends with quite a few neighborhood girls who got allowances and had no problem sharing. My sisters would reciprocate when they could; they all babysat and cleaned houses at early ages.

Bo and I still laugh about the time dad hired us out to dig a 12 x12 well in the ground deep enough to strike water. He dropped us off at 6:00 a.m. several mornings, and each day we had no food or drink until early evening when dad would come to collect us. The funny part is that the homeowner would station his German shepherd at the perimeter of the hole to watch us. Each time the dog didn't hear the rhythm of the pick and shovel, he would growl and bare his teeth.

One day Bo had enough and tried to escape, running into an old dump truck with no doors. The dog chased him through one door and out the other, biting the heel off one of his BF Goodrich sneakers. My brother had business right back in our ditch. We couldn't call for the homeowner because he was at work with my dad.

I remember our dad dropping Bo and me off at the fields at seven in the morning, and we would hoe weeds until five o'clock in the evening with no food. Our dad would come back with a Pepsi for us and raise hell because we were dragging ass. He'd snatch the hoe from us, almost pulling our arms out of socket, and start hoeing a hundred miles an hour for about thirty seconds.

Then he'd hand the hoe back and say, "That's how you do it."

Sure, if you hadn't been there all day. Of course we wouldn't dare say that aloud because we'd have been hospitalized.

My dad always said: *Get in good with the right people that can do you some good.*

He was referring to White people, and he made it his business to do just that. Knowing the right people, he acquired the BH Club—a beer garden with a kitchen and a second-floor apartment—along with at least ten houses. My dad didn't acquire everything he had just by hard work and equal opportunity. There was no such thing. He was given breaks by White men—Jewish men—who liked him and were not afraid to admit their White privilege by giving a hand up. Later in life, I would experience that same thing.

I slaved at the club and in the fields for no payment. By the time I was the senior field hand, so to speak, Bo had gone off to college. When I would ask dad for some money for my labors, he would say: *You live here for free, and I buy the eats.*

All of the houses that he owned and rented out were better than the house we lived in. They were in Martins Ferry, but not across the tracks and down by the river. They were in the nicer part of town and rented mostly by White people; two houses were rented by Black people. Mother would beg him for years to live in one of them. Don't get me wrong, our house in Rayland that we lived in stood out in the neighborhood with its manicured lawn and white-picket-fence—my father always said: *Always put on a front.*

But that well-groomed house would flood almost every fall and get completely submerged except for the attic. So our parents would have to relocate us kids somewhere. Both Uncle John and our grandparents lived on high ground, but not once did they offer to take some of us in, even just overnight. None of our other relatives who lived in nearby towns could be bothered with us either. The same thing happened when my father kicked Bo out of the house when he was a senior in high school. The only place he could go was grandmother's house; she made him stay in an empty root cellar with no water, electricity, or heat and charged him $20 a month. Go figure.

Anyway, my mother had a distant cousin up Narrows Road where the girls and the little kids would go during floods. Bo, Robert, and I would stay in the attic of our flooded house. The trap door to the attic was in the ceiling of our sisters' room. I remember fishing down into our sisters' room. We used to hang out the attic window, watching motorboats riding by with the water about six feet below the window. You'd think that one of those boats would stop and ask if we needed rescuing, even though we weren't looking to be rescued. No such thing.

The flood would usually crest in the middle of the night and disappear by the following day. We couldn't swim, but we weren't afraid of the house floating away because we had huge cables in the basement bolted to the rafters and buried in the concrete floor. When the flood subsided everyone returned home to clean the house, the basement, move all of the furniture back to the house and move all the canned goods back to the basement. The chickens had to fend for themselves, but they instinctively found high ground.

My dad was a friend with the county judge, county health inspector, Martins Ferry chief of police, and most of the policemen. Dad stored beer in the garage in Rayland. When I was thirteen I had to load the truck and drive beer to Martins Ferry. On my way there an Ohio State Trooper noticed the truck swaying; it was out of alignment from years of overcarrying loads of coal, scrap iron, produce, etc.

The trooper pulled me over, and all I saw was a 6'5" trooper with a big gun, big black boots, and a big hat. The first thing I did was start crying uncontrollably. He spent most of his time trying to get me to stop crying. I explained where I was going, what I was hauling, and that *my dad made me do it*. He said he couldn't send me back, and since I was so close to my destination, so he would follow me to my dad's club.

When we arrived he got out of his car, gave me a citation, and said, "Don't let me catch you driving again; your dad should know better."

I went into the club and told my dad what had happened and that we had to go to court the following week.

He said, "To hell with that ticket and to hell with court."

He made me drive the truck back home the same day. It was the longest drive of my life. I just knew that the same trooper would get me again on the way home. I was a nervous wreck; all I could think of was going to jail.

On court day my dad called me to drive the truck to him in Martins Ferry, where the county court was located. When I arrived it was almost time for the hearing. I had to appear before Judge Oakley, who was a legend for jailing people.

But my dad announced, "I'm not going nowhere."

I begged him, cried, and begged him some more, but he wouldn't budge. So I walked uptown and went to court by myself.

There was just the judge and me in the courtroom. He kept looking at me, not speaking, seeming annoyed. I guess because there was no adult with me. He finally asked me where my dad was. I said that he refused to come.

He said, "You take your ass down that hill and get your dad, or I'll throw both of your asses in jail."

I cried all the way to the club to get my dad. I begged him again and again, and he said: *Hell no!* But after I sat crying for a while, he finally said to get in the damn car. We went into the courtroom and again were the only ones there besides the judge, who commenced yelling and cursing at my dad. He asked why in hell he let me drive without a license and said he was going to throw us both in jail. Now I was really crying and scared out of my wits.

My dad replied: "You go straight to hell."

Before I could get my breath, the judge said, "Who won the money in last night's game?"

My father in his club in 1961

Not another word was spoken again about the citation. That's knowing the right people.

When I was fourteen I was tending bar while my dad ran to the liquor store. A guy I wasn't familiar with sat at the bar and asked for a beer. After I served him his Iron City, he asked me how old I was. Of course I said fourteen.

He slapped his badge on the bar. Stop serving. This place is now closed!"

He was from the state liquor board. When my dad got back, I exclaimed why everyone was gone and handed him the written order. He studied it for a little while, unlocked the front door, and switched the open sign back on. He went to see the same judge who dismissed the traffic ticket the next day, and it was business as usual again.

My dad ran poker games after hours in the club basement, sometimes on weeknights and religiously on Friday nights. There would be four to five cloth-covered tables, all occupied. My dad would wear a visor and gartered shirtsleeves, going table to table, taking his cut from each pot. Who do you think would be serving drinks and beer? Yours truly, still fourteen. Guess who would be at those tables gambling? The judge, chief of police, policemen, and county health inspector, in addition to a few regular patrons and some club owners from Wheeling, West Virginia, across the river. Ninety-nine percent of those men were White, and so was my dad's clientele. I would experience this same scenario in the future in a club that I would own in West Virginia.

Seeing all the money on those tables upset me. I didn't understand why in hell we were always doing without—no food in the house other than what we grew and canned, no proper clothing, or toiletries and female necessities for my mother and sisters. It was because my father always preached self-preservation: take care of yourself first.

Not only did he run gambling tables, he was a compulsive gambler. Poker was his game. All of his friends called him Easy Money. I guess he would win easy and lose even easier. He worked with mostly Greeks who were gamblers. He would go to the company store and get twenty-five to fifty cartons of cigarettes against his pay, take them to predominantly Greek Yorkville, Ohio, and sell them for less than he paid for them to get poker money. He gambled with everything: our two hunting dogs, a garden tractor, shot guns, and anything else he could get his hands on

When I was about ten, I decided to steal a pack of my dad's Lucky Strike cigarettes. There were dozens of cartons, so I figured he wouldn't miss one pack. I called my best friend Mike McDaniels to come over. We crawled under the side porch and began puffing two at a time.

My dad arrived from work, saw smoke billowing up through the spaces between the floorboard, and thought the house was on fire. He immediately grabbed the water hose, then once he realized it was me smoking cigarettes, he dragged me out by the hair and beat me with his belt, buckle included, while he had a cigarette hanging from his mouth. During the beating, he forced two cigarettes into my mouth and made me eat them. I guess the lesson he was sending was: Do as I say, not as I do. After eating the cigarettes I was sick as a dog, could hardly breathe, and my throat was swollen. No school the following day.

My dad was also an abuser, just like his dad. He would beat you at the drop of a hat. He would come home in the wee hours or the next morning after he lost at gambling and would start an argument with our mother because he was broke again. He'd hit our mother if she argued back. We'd jump in between them to protect our mother from being hit, and he would beat the hell out of us too. I remember him pulling a gun on my mother several times at home for arguing back and even in public at his club, where she worked all day cooking, waiting, and bussing tables. She may have commented about one of his girlfriends who was always present in the club. Since Bo was the oldest boy, he caught the most hell. Bo always had something to say back, which was like pouring gas on fire.

When I was about twelve, the boys in the neighborhood started the Sixteen Club. When you turned sixteen you had to go into your house, step in your father's way, and bump into him until he asked what the hell you were doing. Then you had to say: *Someone is leaving this house, and it isn't going to be me.*

The first one up was Skippy McDaniels, who lived across the street. His brother Mike was my best friend. There were at least twenty guys trying to find a window where they could watch. What they saw was Skip get the hell beat out of him. He came out of the house limping and crying.

It was Bo's turn next. Again, after he went into the house, the rest of us gathered outside, looking through the windows. My dad was already an abuser and knew a thousand ways to hurt you. But even knowing that Bo prodded my dad and pushed him a little bit a couple of times, then said: *Someone is going to leave the house, and it isn't going to be me.*

My dad picked up a chair and broke it over my brother's back as if he were in a movie. Bo went to the floor and crawled out to the porch, his nose bleeding and in excruciating pain. We picked him up, put him on our homemade stretcher, and took him to our hideout under the bridge. After that the club disbanded.

You could tell if Dad won at gambling because he might give Mother a few dollars for groceries and some extra money to hold on to. Sometimes he also gave us a dollar or two and told us not to spend it, then leave the house to go gamble some more. We were all afraid to spend the money; too many times he had come home wanting his money back because he'd lost at gambling again.

In my younger years I wouldn't pocket a single dime on the sly when working in the club or peddling his produce. I had a paper route that Bo handed down to me, and most of the time, Dad took my profit *and* the money owed to the paper man. I wanted my dad to do well and have the wealth some of my peers' families had. And yeah, I wanted to be accepted and loved.

All of our neighbors thought we had it good. If they only knew what went on behind closed doors. We all had too much pride to tell friends and teachers anything. It was embarrassing to have the furniture company come and repossess the furniture a couple of times, thanks to dad's gambling. My dad always said to keep a front, which meant to never let people see the real you.

I was lucky enough to sometimes get some spending money by helping Mr. Burdess with his peach and strawberry farm. He taught me how to use his walk-behind tractor that had an assortment of attachments, like a harrow I used in between the rows of strawberries to cut up the weeds. I also would attach a front-mounted cutter bar to cut the high grass and weeds in the peach orchard. Working for Mr. Burdess was fun because I had some automation, and I actually got some pay. But it wasn't an everyday job, so I stayed broke most of the time.

When I did get paid, I would give most of it to my mother for food. Other than that, I had to slave for my father for no money. Our mother was just like one of us kids; she didn't have any more money than we did. If you made twenty cents emptying one of the neighbor's trash cans, you bought her an ice cream cone if you bought one for yourself. It hurts me today, thinking how my mother did without, at times having less than we kids did.

Thank God for her mother, who would visit and give Mom a couple of dollars once in a while. When I was little, Grandmother Goldie would always give me a penny. She and my mother would sit on the porch and talk while my mother snapped green beans fresh out of the garden. I'd sit at their feet, playing with my toy glass car, feeling so warm and protected.

I once put a penny in my mouth while sitting at their feet, and it got lodged in my throat, and I couldn't breathe, couldn't speak, and could barely move. They raised one of my arms and pounded my back. The penny didn't come out, but I was able to swallow it. Had I been out in the yard playing, I never would have made it to my mother. That was the first time I almost met my maker.

My dad would tell us to shut up if we cried when he beat us. But if you didn't cry when he was beating you, he'd taunt you. *You think that you are a man now and won't cry, huh?* These beatings would not end until he got tired, no matter what our reactions were.

Some beatings you never forget because they leave a lifetime mark on your body and mind. I'm guessing. Once when I was fourteen, my dad told me to cut the grass. We had a big yard, especially the side yard that was about twenty yards wide and fifty yards deep. We had no lawnmower, so I had to use a hand sickle, which was normally used for cutting hay or grain. Then I'd have to rake up the cuttings with a garden rake, not a leaf rake. I started cutting at about eight in the morning. During the day friends would pass by, trying to talk me into going to play softball. I worked nonstop until four-thirty, then figured I would take a break, go play ball, then finish the grass later that evening since I only had a twelve-by-twelve section left to cut.

I returned home from playing ball about two hours before dark to find my dad sitting on the porch swing with his miner's belt on his lap. It was wide with a large steel buckle, steel hooks, and steel eyeholes to hang accessories. I passed by him as if he weren't waiting for me and went straight to finish cutting the grass. He followed me and started beating me.

"I told you to cut the grass!"

I'd had just about enough, grabbed the belt so he couldn't continue hitting me, and yelled that our neighbors owned power mowers. Since he couldn't swing the belt, he grabbed the rake, which had a weathered wooden handle. I took off running, and he followed, swinging the rake, hitting me on the right leg. As I was limping away, he broke the handle over my back. Throughout life I would hear old Black folks say they got beaten like a mule. I wonder if he treated us like we were mules or was emulating his father.

Bo and I weren't the only two that got horsewhipped by the old man; three of my sisters were beaten several times by him throughout their years in the nest. Everyone got hit by my mother, though usually with a small switch—no big deal. But our dad would beat you until he got tired, take a break, and then continue where he left off. Or he would try to run you off the road.

When I was a junior in high school, my dad told me to take the truck with a load of beer from our house to his club in Martins Ferry. He stressed I was to go straight there, and he'd be right behind me shortly. My girlfriend—later my first wife—lived mid-way en route to the club. I decided to swing by to drop off a book I wanted to give her. I figured what my father didn't know wouldn't hurt anything.

I put my right signal on well in advance before the turn off to my girlfriend's house. As I was getting ready to turn, my dad came out of nowhere, flying up on my right side, slamming his new Pontiac Catalina into the right side of the truck several times, making me go out of control. The truck was already hard to steer because the front-end was out of line. We went from one side of the highway to the other. Luckily there was no oncoming traffic on the two-way highway. To my left was a steep hill with jagged rocks; to my right was the Ohio River waited at the bottom of a hill. I could have been killed. Him too. He caused extensive body damage to both vehicles—all just to keep me from going to her house. This was another one of the reasons why Bo and I thought that he was crazy.

###

For some reason my grandmother didn't like my mother. She called her the baby factory. None of my immediate family was ever accepted as equals by my dad's relatives—until some of us became successful later in life; then they tried to own us as equals.

As a kid my younger siblings and I would sometimes go to my grandmother's yard on Sundays for an after-church meal attended by uncles, aunts, older cousins, and cousins of our age. But we were not invited or wanted by any of them. One day my grandmother told us that our mother was calling us to go home.

When we got home, our mother got upset. "If you didn't hear me call for you, then how did she hear me? Don't go up there anymore on Sundays because you aren't wanted."

I have never forgiven any of them or had anything to do with those cousins, uncles, and aunts since then.

Even though my grandmother didn't like my mother or us kids, she had no problem asking my mother to write her letters or have us kids run errands. And she always helped herself to our vegetable gardens. I suppose the whole town helped themselves to our gardens since they were so huge and far away from our house. When my grandmother was on her death bed after a stroke and cancer, my mother was the one who took care of her because her own children—who all lived nearby—couldn't be found.

I have no idea how my mother did it after the way we were treated. My mother was a saint for tolerating it. When my siblings and I were older, we thought we understood why we weren't accepted by our grandmother and some of her children. She believed that someone in our family was stealing her Social Security check, cashing it, and spending it. How in hell could it be any of us young kids. And our older siblings didn't have bank accounts. They wouldn't have the nerve anyways.

Many years later we found out the culprit was Cousin Johnny, the boy who had everything, including his own bank account. In 2015 I took my high school basketball coach out to lunch. He'd also been one of Johnny's teachers and said my cousin was constantly in trouble for stealing anything that wasn't locked down. He was a kleptomaniac and even got kicked out of college for stealing. But my grandmother probably went to her grave believing my family was stealing from her.

Almost none of our neighbors showed any prejudice that we could detect, especially the McDanielses. Mrs. McDaniels was a registered nurse, and Mr. McDaniels was a steel worker. Their son Mike was my best friend from first grade up until ninth grade—that's when he started dating. Then he dropped me like a hot rock. White girls were off-limits for my brothers and me. Playing house was okay as young kids but a no-no as teens. Again, we were the only Black family in junior high and high school when I was growing up. All my friends were Caucasian, but we parted ways when it came to girls, the community pool, the skating rink, the golf course, etc., because no Blacks were allowed. Catching the school bus was not an equal opportunity either. The bus would pick up the White kids who lived on our street in front of their houses, but the Holmeses had to walk or run a half-mile to catch the same bus at a pickup point in the center of town.

Even though Mike and I were no longer inseparable, we stayed cordial in high school because we played football, basketball, and baseball together. We also both attended West Liberty State College. He was a year ahead of me. One cold February weekend we'd both gone home to visit, and Mike said I could hitch a ride back to college with him and his friend, who I was familiar with because he'd gone to high school with us. But when the friend showed up, and Mike opened the back door for me to get in, the guy asked what I was doing.

"I'm going with you guys."

He shook his head. "You aren't going in my car."

Mike got in and left me standing there as they drove off. Mrs. McDaniels happened to be looking out of her kitchen window, so she came out and asked me what happened. I told her, and she went ballistic. She couldn't believe her son would stay in the car with someone like that. She went back in the house, called out at work, then came back outside and told me to get into the car. She insisted on driving me back to school and was steaming the whole way. When we arrived she parked at Mike's dorm and told me to follow her in. I explained I wasn't allowed; no Blacks were allowed.

"They are right now," she said.

She went to Mike's room and slammed the door open. Mike, his friend the driver, and three other guys were smoking cigars, drinking, and playing cards. Mike was leaning back on the rear legs of the chair, and his mother kicked the chair out from beneath him, causing him to crash onto the floor.

"I can't believe that you rode back here with him," she yelled, pointing at the driver, "after he left your friend standing there!" I am ashamed of you, and you should be ashamed of yourself. I can't believe that you're the son that I raised."

We left, and she dropped me off, still apologizing. Another time Mr. McDaniels urged Bo to go see his friend, who was a construction foreman about a job. But when Bo applied for the job using Mr. McDaniels as a reference, the foreman said, "We don't hire your kind." Mr. McDaniels got a lesson that day about his friend.

Our next-door neighbor Mrs. Biggars was probably in her eighties. She had long, white hair down to her waist, skin pale as snow, and sharp features that made her look like a witch. She had a monster pet raccoon on her back porch on a leash, and it lived in a large basket. She also had the most beautiful front lawn that we loved to play in at night when we thought that she'd be asleep. One night when we were playing in her yard, she came out on her porch with her pistol blazing.

When you're shot at point-blank, your knees turn to butter. You feel like you are trying to escape in slow motion. It doesn't help if your older brother is knocking everyone down in his way. Ten of us ran behind our house crying because Bo and Skippy McDaniels were missing. We thought that they were dead. But there was a full moon that night, and we finally saw their silhouettes high up in a tree on the hillside by grandfather's house. It was hard to believe that she didn't hit anyone.

It seemed that every full moon, she'd come out after midnight, ringing a cowbell and firing her pistol. Every time she fired her pistols, the police would confiscate them. That lady must have had a lot of pistols. Other times late at night, she'd stand on her back porch, ringing her very loud cowbell and combing her long hair, laughing like a witch.

We played softball on Narrows Road, and sometimes the ball would accidentally go into her yard. She'd run out, grab the ball, take it in the house, and throw it in her pot belly stove to burn it up. One time she burned Mike's new softball, and we told Mrs. McDaniels what happened. She gave us one of those rubber balls to hit in the yard intentionally. Mrs. Biggars came out, picked up the ball, and threw it in her stove. But this time black smoke started billowing out her chimney, then out of her windows. She came out of the house gagging and choking. After that Mrs. Biggars never bothered our softballs anymore.

One day her pet raccoon broke loose and was in our backyard, foaming at the mouth. Dad said it was rabid. The Burdess's big collie was in our yard and chased the raccoon to the creek. Dad told me to go get the shotguns; we needed to kill the raccoon before it bit one of the neighborhood kids. I had a 20-gauge, and dad had a 12-gauge shotgun. We walked slowly through the woods, and I was about thirty feet in front of my dad. I heard a loud hiss, and by the time I looked up, the raccoon had leaped down from a tree to attack me. My dad shot it in midair before it could land on my head. What a shot.

Eventually, Mrs. Biggars flipped out, and the neighbors watched as authorities put her in a straitjacket and strapped her to a gurney as she yelled and struggled to get free. We never saw her again.

Many of our dogs met their maker because we lived near two roads: Narrows Road and State Route 7. I was also hit by a car—twice. The first time was when I was in third grade. I chased a ball without looking for traffic and ended up on the windshield of the oncoming car. I had minor cuts, bruises, and scratches and ached all over. That was the second time that I almost met my maker.

A year later I was hit again while riding my bicycle. I was knocked off of the bike, skidding down the highway and peeling the skin off my elbows, arms, knees, and hip. I looked like a raw piece of meat. There would be many more near-death events. Over the years when I'd tell people how many times that I escaped death, most of them said God has a plan for me. That may be so, but I wish I had a hint of what the plan is.

The best thing about Narrows Road was when it snowed. It became impossible to drive on unless you had chains or studs in your tires. Cars with bare tires attempting to climb the hill slipped and slid all over the road, barely advancing. We helped push cars to the top, and most of the drivers would tip us fifty cents, or once in a blue moon, a dollar. That same road was also our sledding hill, riding trail, and bicycle/go-kart racetrack. We would race across Rte. 7 and end up in Mr. Burdess's huge side yard.

###

Many of our White friends dropped out of school to work in coal mines or steel mills. My dad wanted Bo and me to quit school and work for him. You know how that would have turned out: we'd be working for free. What kind of signal was that for a man who took us out of the ghetto? There had been plenty of times we wanted to quit school but because we didn't have nepotism like the White boys. Those who did not drop out of high school had summer jobs in construction or at steel mills, while we could not get hired. Keep in mind that Bo was almost four years older than me, so I've been working like a man alongside Bo since I was nine or ten years old.

During our early teenage years, we were very industrious and inventive when it came to making up and playing games. The whole neighborhood would pitch in with shovels and picks to make a baseball field out of an abandoned cornfield. We did the same for football. When Mr. Burdess stopped growing peaches and uprooted all of his fruit trees, he let the neighborhood boys build a bicycle racetrack on a part of the former orchard.

Bo and his friend Bo Selman, Mr. Burdess's grandson, opened a bicycle repair shop right in the middle of the track. They sponsored my brother Robert's bike, which had long lug nuts on the back wheels designed to tear out the spokes of the competition, which the two Bos could profit from by fixing the broken spokes.

We weren't as advanced as the teenagers of today who play video games, get drunk, hang out in the malls, and God knows whatever else. The whole neighborhood of boys and girls would go pick strawberries at five cents a basket, pool their money together, buy loads of junk food—lunch meat, cookies, candy, bread, soda pop, potato chips, moon pies, cheese doodles, etc.—then have a party in my basement, which was the neighborhood hangout. We'd eat until we got sick.

In the winter we'd play outside in the snow until midnight on weekends—sledding, kick the can, and fox and geese were our favorites. In the summer we built rafts out of tree logs and float from the creek behind our house all the way to the mouth of the Ohio River, which was about two miles away. Most of our fun took place at night because during the day, especially in the summer, we were busy in the vegetable fields or slaving for our dad.

My paternal grandfather was a church-going man, but he was also an abuser. He would beat my grandmother and threaten her with a gun. My dad had to run up there several times to take the gun away. Like father, like son.

In the back of my grandfather's house was a big grape arbor—a structure for the vines to grow on. At night us neighborhood boys would go there and fill up on grapes. One night we either made too much noise, or he was waiting for us. Grandfather came out on his porch, and we were all lying on our backs because that was the best way you could see the grapes against the moonlight. He couldn't see us, so he shot at random in the dark, hoping to hit us. First he shot at us with a BB gun, which was no big deal. He next shot at us several times with his rifle, and it quickly became serious, with bullets ricocheting all over the rocks around us. Then my grandfather fired a shotgun, causing the whole porch to light up. How ignorant. We all got the hell out of there—I lost my cap in the process—and ran through the thickets, with briars ripping our arms and faces. We ran through the woods in the dark all the way to the next town,

Tiltonsville, then circled back home using the street.

The following morning Bo and I were in bed when we heard grandfather's voice. Moments later our dad came into the room and asked me where my Cleveland Indians baseball cap was. Well, you know the rest. He beat us, belt buckle and all, until he got tired. He took a breather and then continued to beat us. Like father, like son. When I finally dared to go into the living room and retrieve my hat, the little knob on the top of the cap was half shot off. He could have killed me. That was another time I almost met my maker.

Later that day my grandfather was sitting on his back porch. From there he could see our house and was watching Mike and me playing catch in the street. I saw him point his rifle at us as if he were going to shoot us. We ducked down behind a stone wall that bordered Mr. Hannah's yard. Every time we stuck our heads up to see if he were still there, he would aim at us again. We couldn't call for our parents because they weren't home. This went on for about three hours, and finally the town constable, Mr. Sudsberry, drove by. We hailed him, and he pulled over. Still hiding, we pointed toward grandfather and said he was going to shoot us. He asked us what we did to deserve getting shot, and we told him about stealing grandfather's grapes the night before.

Mr. Sudsberry said, "Good for you," and drove off.

Shortly after that my grandfather went into the house, and we escaped. We never did tell our parents, especially Mike because he would have gotten a good beating if he told his dad why we were pinned down.

Even though I was somewhat of a loner in high school, I was pretty popular due to my athletic ability. And I sang a couple of songs at Senior Night a week before graduation. A local Black band from Martins Ferry that sometimes played in Dad's club sometimes allowed me to bust a tune, so I recommended them for Senior Night, and our class advisor went with them. I saw how crazy the girls were over singers like Elvis, the Beach Boys, Bobby Darin, etc. I was actually a little shy in those days but got up there and sang in hopes of landing a girlfriend on the down-low—no such luck. Can you blame a guy for dreaming?

I had one true White friend in high school, Regis Woods, who lived in Glen Robbins, which was only about four miles away from Rayland but years behind; Regis's town had outhouses and no running water. He used to stay over at my house, and we'd sleep on the porch in the summer, camp in the woods, play by the Ohio River, shoot crows for the sport, and go rabbit hunting, which was one of our favorite pastimes. None of my other so-called friends that I played sports with ever invited me to their house, to their parties, or to just hang out.

Regis double-dated with me for the junior prom; it was unheard of for a White couple double dating with two Black kids in 1961 in that Ohio town in the presence of the whole White student body and faculty. Regis was different than the rest because he had his own mind, so peer pressure was not part of his life. Regis went to college, became a teacher, did some coaching, climbed up the ladder, and eventually became superintendent of schools at Cambridge, Ohio. Regis and I have been friends for more than sixty-five years, and we still keep in touch.

My lifelong friend
Reggie Wood (#52)

###

When the Marine Corps recruiter came to the high school to convince seniors to join up, I went along but had no intention of joining. I had no desire to kill Vietnamese people. For a long time I was looking for sports to get me out of Rayland and out from under my father's thumb. Neither Bo nor I particularly loved playing sports, but we had a natural ability that enabled us to excel. Bo went to West Liberty State College with no scholarship, but since he played football and track, the college's head of the Physical Education department, Dr. Blatnik, arranged a place for him to stay on campus—blacks were not allowed in the dorms—and a work-study job doing maintenance.

During my senior year in high school, I received letters from a few major colleges and was all set to go to talk with Ohio State football coach Woody Hayes. Two of my coaches were driving me. I was going to wear one of Bo's suits, but he came home from college that week and refused to let me. It was like my dad all over again. Even though my brother had no love for our dad, he was just like him at times.

Too embarrassed to admit I had nothing appropriate to wear and why, I stood them up to go duck hunting. Then I stayed home for three days or so, afraid to face my coaches and so ashamed I considered quitting school. When I finally returned to school, not a word was said to me by either coach. A couple of years later, I found out that one of my older sisters answered the door when they'd come to get me and told the coaches what had happened that night before.

After I graduated, Dr. Blatnik talked me into going to West Liberty State at the last minute. I got tuition, a free stay in the dingy barracks that Bo lived in, and a $30 a month work-study job. I had to pay for my food and books. It was a far cry from what I would have gotten from Ohio State—a full ride with no Jim Crow. I wondered what kind of brother would begrudge his younger brother that opportunity.

I received a birthday card from Woody Hayes in both my freshman and sophomore years. If I hadn't been so backward, I would have taken the hint and contacted Mr. Hayes during my freshman year at West Liberty State, even if it meant having to contact my former high school football coach to do the leg work. Well, that's water over the falls. After sixty-two years, I still wonder if it was jealousy over me possibly attending Ohio State and doing better than him that made Bo act the way he did or if it was because he'd worked so hard to get those clothes that he just wasn't going to share no matter what. It still bothers me today, but I hold no grudge. After thinking back about how I let my pride get in the way of asking my coaches for help before and after the proposed Ohio State visit, I don't blame my brother. I blame myself.

I often wondered why I still looked up to my brother. I'm no psychiatrist, but maybe I was looking to be accepted and loved no matter how hard the road was to travel—misery loves company. And Bo may have felt the same way about our father, no matter how badly he was treated.

FOLLOWING THE FOOTSTEPS

While in college Bo had been going to Cleveland in the summers to work with another Uncle John, this one married to my mother's sister. Uncle John worked at Republic Steel and had a small home improvement business on the side. The summer before I started at West Liberty State, I followed my brother again, this time to Cleveland to work with Uncle John. Bo and I had to share a basement apartment with our mother's brother, Uncle Harold, who also worked for Republic Steel during the week, then spent weekends at his home in Martins Ferry. Even though Uncle Harold was already paying the apartment's rent, Uncle John also charged Bo and me rent as well—triple-dipping, so to speak. Another great experience with my relatives.

Bo earned a few dollars more a week than me but not much more. I earned enough to pay rent, eat a snack for lunch, and go roller skating once a week. I was able to purchase a couple of shirts, pants, a pair of shoes, some socks, a sweater, and a jacket. Even though I was still only surviving, I was happy and felt like a rich man, happy to be away from my dad. After a whole summer of work, I had about $250 saved for food and books, which wasn't nearly enough. Just like Bo, I struggled through college, but I was determined.

We were two country boys in the big city, and Uncle John always tried to embarrass us by quizzing us on the Bible or asking stupid questions in general. He was a Southern country boy himself who had done pretty well for himself. I guess that he thought that we weren't going anywhere in life, so we let him have his insults. He also often told us that we needed to come and work for him. We weren't dumb enough to fall for his offer of full-time employment because we would be working for peanuts, and we both knew what we wanted, no matter what obstacles were in our way.

During that same summer I got to meet a few new friends, including the girl of my dreams, Gayle. She was petite with freckles, golden-brown skin, and long hair. I became friends with Uncle John's half-brother, Charles, who also worked with us, had graduated from the same gigantic high school where she was now a senior. He tried for a couple of years to get next to her, as he would say, but no luck—just friends.

Charles was a little guy who looked the nerd type, very soft-spoken, and religious. I was six foot two at that time, full of muscles, and an accomplished athlete. I wasn't hard to look at either. When Charles introduced Gayle to me, I could tell it was over for both of us. I asked for her phone number, and without hesitation she gave it to me. Her family was upper-middle class who lived in the suburbs. Her father was the band director at that same high school; he also had a studio in his basement where he gave private music lessons. The mother owned a beauty parlor.

Going to their house was like going to my dream home. Gayle had a younger brother who was very caught up in city life, a real hipster who could play just about any instrument. He gave me one of his electric guitars as a gift and taught me how to play a few chords.

Her parents liked me. After we had become puppy love sweethearts—a peck on the cheek and at most a pucker with lips barely touching—her dad took the three of us to the movies, dropped us off, gave us admission and refreshment money, and picked us up after the movie. He did the same for the amusement park and the outdoor skating rink. It was like a dream come true. It reminded me how my White friends lived back in Rayland. I'm guessing Gayle's brother was always tagging along as a chaperone, but it didn't matter. I had nothing but good intentions for her. Besides, I had no idea what bad intentions were anyway.

My senior year in high school, running for a touchdown after a pass reception

As a senior I was chosen to play in the Ohio vs. West Virginia all-star game. Her whole family drove all the way from Cleveland to watch the game. Her dad felt like a father coming to see me play, which I never experienced before. After the game they took me out for a late-night snack then dropped me off at home in Rayland. This relationship continued on into college.

I spent the summer after graduating from high school working for my uncle John, then went off to my freshman year in college. Bo was a senior. We both reported to football camp in late August 1961 for double sessions, which seemed like a piece of cake because it meant two weeks of three meals a day. I was competing against three freshmen and a senior who'd been a starter for three years for the tight-end position. Little did our teammates know that they had to compete against two hardened and maybe angry ex-slaves. I was stronger, faster, and had hands like glue for catching passes. Needless to say, I knocked a three-year starter out of his tight end position.

Bo played offensive tackle and lined up next to the tight end. When we were on the field together, we drove the defensive tackle back to the next town, making a hole wide enough to drive a dump truck through. I kind of felt sorry for the guys we had to block.

Once double sessions were over and classes started, there wouldn't be any more free meals, and I was on my own. Going to classes with no breakfast and no lunch, then off to a strenuous practice was déjà vu. After practice, I went to work-study, which could be anything: digging a ditch for a broken water line, shoveling snow, and sweeping floors. In the winter we sometimes had to plow snow on campus. Bo drove an old dump truck while I operated the jack to control the blade and tilt the blade manually. After work Bo and I would pitch in for Dinty Moore stew, pork and beans, SpaghettiOs, or even just a large bowl of corn flakes. Pretty hard to study with a half-empty stomach. It took determination.

Me, running the football my freshman year in college

In the spring random apple trees growing around campus helped fill the stomach voids. Some days, the apples were the only food we had. During holiday recesses we stayed on campus, and the head of maintenance would find some work for us to get a few dollars for survival.

Because I had a physical education minor, I was required to take a swimming class. Dr. Blatnik was the professor, but a student taught the class for credits. The student teaching that term played on our football team. I thought: *Hell, I have it made.*

The class only met once a week. We'd have to tread water, and I'd inconspicuously hang onto the side of the pool because I had a fear of water. He told us to breaststroke, and I'd tell him to go to hell. He told us to butterfly, and again I would tell him to go to hell. I wasn't worried about the grade because my teammate would pass me.

You would have thought I would want to learn to swim, considering I had almost drowned while in high school. My friend Billy and I were out on the Ohio River fishing in his little flat-bottom aluminum boat when a big barge passed by, leaving a wake about three feet high. We didn't know that we were supposed to steer into the waves. Instead, we steered with the waves, and the water came over the side of the boat, causing it to sink. The water was too deep to walk out, so I dog paddled as long as I could. Then I started struggling, fighting for my life.

Out of nowhere a motorboat showed up. A White lady and a man were in the boat a few yards away. But I had too much pride to yell for help even though I was drowning. I blame that on the old man constantly telling us to always put on a front. Still doggie paddling, the couple were debating whether or not I needed help. I could hear the lady insisting that I needed help while the man insisted that I could swim because he thought the oars floating beside me were water skis.

"If he can't swim, what is he doing way out here?"

The lady could see through my crazy pride and insisted that he go over to me and pick me up. When they came close, I almost upset their boat climbing in. We all thought that Billy had drowned, but they found him on a big peer that barges tied onto near the shore. Thank God for that lady, and thank God Billy knew how to swim. That near-death experience hadn't stuck.

On the final day Dr. Blatnik walked in, announced he was leading the class, and told everyone to go jump in the deep end of the pool and tread water for five minutes. I thought it was a piece of cake because I could doggie paddle and grab on the side without him seeing. After five minutes, it's my group's turn to do the breaststroke for one lap. Talk about panic. I had played around all that semester and couldn't swim a lick. But instead of making an excuse by saying that I had a bad cramp or something, I did the stupid thing and jumped in. As soon as I hit the water, I started swimming for my life with my eyes closed and holding my breath.

I could hear the screaming laughter echoing in the empty stadium. Apparently, I was splashing in circles and going no place. But I was still in the, running out of gas, and figured I could walk out. I went down but couldn't touch the bottom. I came back up fighting, the laughter louder. I couldn't fight anymore and went under. No more laughter. I couldn't breathe, and everything started turning grey.

I felt tugging on my body and hair, then found myself gagging and choking on the side of the pool with many guys staring down at me. After I regained my strength, I found out a guy named Moe Burke saved my life. Dr. Blatnik chewed me out in front of the entire class.

"You will stay here this summer, and you will learn how to swim."

Under my breath I said: *Go to hell*, walked out, and went home for the summer. I received my grades in the mail expecting an F, but to my surprise I received an A. I wouldn't learn to swim until eight or nine years later after I installed a pool in my first house.

I don't mean to put White women on a pedestal, but they played a big part during different stages of my life, some with sympathy or empathy and some helping me in life. A couple of girls who were my classmates in high school visited me on campus once in a while. Karen Piko was very popular in high school, and I once helped her during a confrontation in the parking lot of a local hangout. I guess she never forgot that a Black guy came to her aid when all the White guys stood around doing nothing. The other was Midge Schamahorn, whose mother was our third-grade teacher. We were buddies in elementary school—I sat behind her and played with her pigtails. It felt good that they visited, and I appreciated it.

I'm sure most people on campus knew that the two Black guys lived over the hill in a place just short of a shack, so no other White girl would dare come there. But Karen and Midge visited and asked me if I needed anything and talked about what was happening on campus. They did not worry about being seen with me because they were not afraid to admit they had White privilege. It was no secret to them that we weren't allowed to stay in the dormitory. And even if we had been allowed, we couldn't afford it.

Forty years later I invited about twenty or so former high school classmates, including Karen and Midge, to my house in West Virginia as a mini-reunion for all of us who still lived locally in the Ohio valley.

Everyone was talking about our high school days, and one of my guests said, "Good times, huh, Ken?"

I replied that I had no idea because I wasn't included. Everyone got very quiet.

"Did any of you ever seen me at the community pool, at the roller rink, on the golf course or at any house parties or birthday parties?"

Someone said, "We didn't know that." "How could that be

possible?" I asked. "You were the ones that never invited me anyplace; your parents were the ones that didn't allow me in the places that my dad paid taxes for."

Complete silence. Then I softened the blow by telling them that was the past. "You all were kids, and that's not

My house in West Virginia, on top of my mountain

the reason why I invited you all to my house."

Once my college classes started, I caught a ride with Uncle Harold on his weekly commute so I could visit Gayle. Her parents knew how I struggled in college and offered to help me more than once. Each time I refused politely, even though I badly wanted that help. I thought taking anything from anyone would cause them to look down on me. It was stupid pride, prompted by my dad always saying: *Put on a good front.*

During my sophomore year I caught a ride with Uncle Harold to Cleveland to spend Thanksgiving weekend with her family, staying in a guest room. Gayle and I spent most of our time in the recreation room since it was snowing and freezing outside. We played records all the time on her old player. As I was leaving, I promised I'd see her for Christmas and that I'd buy her a new stereo as a present—even though I didn't have a penny to my name and the holidays would be here too soon.

I went back to college, and while talking to my White teammates on the varsity basketball team, I told them what I had promised my girlfriend for Christmas but didn't know if I could come up with $29.95

by then. They all laughed and told me about King's Jewelry in Wheeling. The store offered any student credit for up to $100, with a payment plan of $10 a month. There were flyers all over campus for the company.

I caught a ride that weekend to go work in my dad's club and got dropped off in Wheeling, which was en route to Martins Ferry. I went into the jewelry store and asked about the credit program with the flyer in my hand. The gentleman at the counter asked me if I had a steady job. I showed him my college ID and told him I had a work-study job on campus and also worked for my father.

He said, "Not enough; we don't give credit."

I was hurt and desperate, so I asked to see his boss or a manager.

"What for? They'll just tell you the same thing."

He finally went into the back of the store and stayed there for quite a long time. He and his boss finally came out; the boss confirmed no credit and then added insult.

"What is it that you didn't understand about what my worker said?"

Had I been raised differently, I would have told him to kiss where the sun didn't shine.

After that weekend I went back to campus and told some of my teammates what had happened. They called it bullshit, and one of the guys offered to get the stereo, and I could pay him back. But I was too hurt and had too much stupid pride and refused. I never bought that stereo, never went back to Cleveland to see Gayle, and never gave her an explanation until forty-one years later at a street reunion in Weirton, West Virginia, where she lived before moving to Cleveland. The town where I resided for fourteen years. My mother told me that for two years, my puppy love girlfriend had come looking for me after I abandoned her. By then I was already married out of feeling sorry for myself, feeling sorry for my new wife, and in the military. After that stupidity, I learned quickly what my dad always said: "Surround yourself with people that can help you."

I did meet with Gayle forty-one years later and apologized. We sat and talked for hours. She told me she'd married, had a daughter, and divorced. Her parents were deceased; her brother had played in big bands for years, including with Les Paul, then committed suicide over an unfaithful wife who got tired of him being on the road so much. Who knows what the future could have been for us?

During my first two years in college, I sometimes caught a ride home in the evenings with a commuter I knew who lived near Rayland, just to go home to get something to eat. I'd also catch a ride to Martins Ferry on weekends to work in the old man's club on Friday until 2:00 or 3:00 a.m., Saturday 8:00 a.m. until 2:00 a.m. again, then Sunday 9:00 a.m. until midnight. For all those hours he paid me a lousy $10 dollars, and then I had to get back to school the best I knew how.

I knew a guy who lived in Martins Ferry who told me anytime I needed a ride back to school, no matter what day or time, he would drive me back. I used him, but the problem with that was he charged $5, half of what I slaved for. That left me five dollars to eat with for a week. Sometimes I subsisted on a Zagnut candy bar and apples picked from the trees on campus. I couldn't wait to have an away game because we always got a pregame meal, and away games gave us a pregame lunch and dinner.

Bo and I had a roommate move in named Bobby Douglass, who was a champion wrestler and a running back. Our college head coach, Mr. Kavolic, had been Douglas's high school wrestling coach and recruited him. I didn't know Bobby's financial situation, but I suspected Coach Kavolic subsidized him because he always had some food to eat, wore nice clothes, and went home pretty often. Bo, a couple of other teammates, and I sometimes teased Bobby by calling Coach Bobby's daddy.

Bobby must have told Coach Kavolik what we were saying because one day before practice, Coach called the whole team to gather around him and talked about the usual pre-practice drills.

Then out of nowhere, he said, "I don't like Ken and Bo Holmes, but they can always play ball for me."

What a slap in the face. How sophomoric or childish was that?

My freshman year I made all-conference, and Bo made second-team all-conference. He also made first-team Little All American, which honored the top players from Division II and III colleges. An example of Jim Crow at its finest, showing how prejudiced the WV conference was. Bo wasn't good enough to make first-team in the local yokel conference, but he made the national first-team. Go figure. I could see that happening because on numerous occasions Bo and I were called nigger by the opponents' fans and by the opposing players on many occasions, I guess to piss us off so we'd get ourselves kicked out of the game. Or maybe that was how they actually felt. I choose the latter. I couldn't help but wonder again why in hell a brother would bring his younger brother into this shit.

Bo was a senior but not in grade points. He finally had enough of hunger and struggling, so he dropped out of college, married his girlfriend, and joined the military. Bobby Douglas, after his sophomore year, transferred to Iowa State University on a full scholarship in wrestling, where he became a legend and wrestled in the Olympics. He later wrote books on wrestling and was a member of the Iowa State faculty. As for me, after my sophomore year, I followed my brother yet again. Like a dumb idiot I married my girlfriend of two years and joined Air Force, where I would get three hot meals, a cot, and the GI bill to pay for college after discharge. I couldn't take being hungry all the time anymore either.

MARRIAGE AND
THE MILITARY LIFE

B ecause I wasn't twenty-one yet, I needed parental approval to get married. My dad wouldn't sign, telling me that I was stupid to get married and wanting me to work for him instead. I asked my mother if I should get married. She thought I should because *two can make it better than one.* Since the old man was wrong in his advice most of the time, I ignored him. My mother signed for me, and I got married. I later wished I had listened to him that one time.

We got married in her brother's house. We had no honeymoon, nor did we consummate the marriage. We sat up all night on her brother's couch, and I shipped out in the morning for Cleveland. After taking my oaths, I headed to Lackland Air Force Base in Texas for basic training. After graduation from training, I was assigned to the Thirty-First Fighter Wing, Intelligence Division at Homestead Air Force Base, Homestead, Florida. I arrived right in the middle of the Cuban crisis. Our job was to keep abreast of targets in Cuba, mainly missile sites, radar sites, and soviet aircraft.

During my downtime while at Homestead, I'd often go play with the flight simulator, which was located directly behind the intelligence office. It was a replica of the F-100 Super Sabre. I became friends with the technicians over there and spent quite a few hours in the cockpit. I had gotten good enough to take off and fly around.

Looking out of the cockpit, you could see a large screen on the wall showing the flying patterns while the technicians gave you instructions. My biggest problem was landing the aircraft. I crashed it many times. When I crashed a siren blared. Landing was difficult because there was no sensation of movement in this particular simulator. You had to know when to pitch up, nose up, flaps down, throttle down, touch down, pop the parachute, and break.

I think I landed once on all the times trying. Being in that cockpit, being with pilots all day every day, listening to their jargon while briefing and debriefing them, made me want to be a pilot too. I promised myself to start taking flying lessons somewhere down the line for a private pilot's license. I took about six lessons on weekends before leaving for overseas.

After being on base for six months, I flew my wife out to Florida since I had a four-day pass. I picked her up at Miami International in the used 1957 Ford Fairlane convertible I'd bought, and we drove back to the base, where I had temporary housing. We were both virgins because I was taught that sex was a no-no before marriage. Our daughter was conceived during that four-day visit. I didn't see my wife until a year later because I was always going somewhere—Spain, Japan, Alaska, etc.—on temporary duty since I was in intelligence.

When I returned to the States, I sent for my wife and my daughter and went on separate rations, meaning I was no longer living on base and was partially compensated for food, housing, and two dependents. I commuted every day and worked a nine-to-five job just like anyone else except I belonged to Uncle Sam and could ship out at any time. A year after she came to be a permanent resident, our son was born.

Florida was different than little Rayland, Ohio. In Florida when you went off base, you'd see signs saying: No Coloreds Allowed. The public bathrooms said *White Women* or *White Men,* and the other sign said *Colored,* which meant that all Black folks had to use the same bathroom. The water fountains were also designated White or Colored. This was all new to me; even though Ohio had its similarities, they hid it better.

One day I was driving with the top down in my new White Chevy Impala convertible past a strip mall in Miami with my daughter in her car seat in the back. As I was passing by a bowling alley, two White girls called out: *Nice car!* There were two White police officers standing by the girls, and I imagined that they were hitting on the girls. I saw the look on their faces when the girls spoke to me, and I knew I was in trouble.

They immediately jumped into their cruiser, followed me, put on flashers, and pulled me over. Through the years this happened to me many times. I was told by my dad to always say sir and be polite when getting pulled over by the police, which I did.

They had me turn on my wipers, brake lights, horn, etc. I told them that the car was new and there shouldn't be any problems. They then went into a private conference, came back, and wrote me a citation for faulty taillights. I didn't know whether to laugh or argue, but I was too smart to go down that path and just said: *Thank you, sir.*

When I went to work on Monday, I went to my commanding officer, Fountain, and told him what had happened, and he was fuming. He and I went to see the base commander to tell my story. The base commander then called the Miami Chief of Police and went off on him. The chief said to rip up the citation and that he would deal with the two officers. I doubt that he reprimanded them, but at least I didn't have to pay the ticket. Keep in mind that this happened in the sixties during martin Luther King's and John Lewis's days of raising hell peacefully. Thank God for them.

Shortly after that I was shipped to Turkey, leaving my wife home alone with the kids. International telephone calls were hard to do and expensive, so I wrote my wife almost every day and sent pictures of my newfound friends, and she sent me pictures of the kids and her in exchange.

Our deployment to Turkey was supposed to be a six-month rotation, but we ended up being there for a year. Without revealing too much I can say that we were there because Turkey was a strategic location during the Cold War. Our job was to brief the pilots on Russian planes, namely the

Mig 21, which was Russia's fastest jet at that time, on the different types of radar, and pertinent targets. The pilots flew sorties every day, practicing over the designated bombing range.

Since we were in intelligence, some of us were authorized to fly in the back seat in one of the jets. I remember getting my first ride in the fighter jet. Colonel McGinnis was the commanding officer of the 306 Fighter Squadron, and he bet the other pilots going up that I would not get sick on my first flight. They took him up on that bet, as did several other pilots sitting around in the command post.

The colonel pulled me to the side. "Holmes, you better not get sick."

"I won't."

Then I took a piece of that action and threw my money into the pot. I was about to find out real soon that there was a big difference between a flight simulator and a real jet.

Takeoff was beautiful watching the jet separate quickly from Earth, with all four pilots asking me if I was okay. I guess they thought I'd get sick just on takeoff since we pulled a couple of negative Gs. Our jet was carrying four five-hundred-pound bombs, one five-hundred-pound napalm bomb, and two thousand rounds of .50 caliber explosive head bullets fired from the canon in the nose of the jet. A trigger for the canon was located right on the joystick. After all the clowning and laughing was over, we were approaching the target, and things got serious.

I was flying with Captain Johnson, who was the lead pilot and flight commander. We went in first. We dove in from about 20,000 feet on a 45-degree angle because we were going to drop one of the bombs. If you think that the world's largest roller coaster was scary, try being in the backseat of a fighter jet pulling positive Gs.

After we dropped the bomb, he slammed the stick all the way back, and we shot straight up in the air like a bullet to get out of the way of the bomb burst. Once at a certain altitude, he slammed the stick back again, almost into the inverted flight, then rolled back over to normal flight, and we got back, so we were fourth in line.

I couldn't believe I was going to have to do this more times. Not good. By the third run I was ready to throw up, but I didn't want to mess up the cockpit. So I took off one of my flight gloves and used it as a barf bag, then folded it and tucked it into one of the pockets of my flight suit. I knew I could not disappoint Colonel McGuiness.

All the pilots kept asking me if I were okay, hoping I would get sick so they could win the jackpot. After everyone expended their ordinance, we formed up and headed back to the base. Again, all of the pilots asked if I was okay, and I answered yes.

Captain Johnson said, "It isn't over yet."

He slammed the stick all the way back, simultaneously popping the plane into the afterburner. I did not know where I was for a second and screamed like a little schoolgirl. The pilots laughed so hard that it seemed that they couldn't control their planes. They all asked again if I was sick.

"No, but do not pull that shit again!" making them break into laughter again. After landing we went back to operations, and the colonel was waiting by the door with my half of the money, teasing the pilots. I got out of there immediately and went back to my room, sick as a dog but with full pockets, and lay down for an hour or so and then went back to the intelligence office.

I flew back seat as an observer in this F-100 Super Sabre fighter jet in Turkey and in Vietnam.

On weekends while in Turkey, I really enjoyed going with friends to downtown Izmir, which was a good-sized city. I loved bartering with the local street vendors. We visited there so often we got to know some of the locals pretty well. Sometimes we'd get a couple of bottles of wine, a loaf of bread, some shish kabob, and find our *arkadas* (friend) Nazif, who was always in town with a horse-drawn wagon full of hay. We sat on his wagon, eating and drinking, taking in the hustle and bustle of the city. There were many carriages for hire, and some of the drivers would occasionally let us take the reins. I loved the ambience of that entire city and had good times there I'll never forget.

When our rotation ended, I sent my wife the date I'd be home. But I was really coming back two days sooner to surprise her and the kids. After landing, I caught a cab home, arriving about 9:30 p.m. I noticed her open the curtains to peek out and thought she'd be running to get the kids out of bed to greet me. I took my key out and opened the front door. No greeting. No kids. But I did see a man running out the back door. She was caught dead to rights. I was shocked.

The children weren't home because she'd had her girlfriend take them for the night, so our big fight went on practically all night. For the next several days, I came home after work, trying not to upset the children. But my wife and I were not talking. I couldn't take it anymore and moved back to the base. I still took care of my responsibilities and visited the kids as often as I could bear coming home and facing her. I filed for a divorce. But when my attorney brought the final papers for me to sign, I tore them up. I guess love is blind. He reminded me of how much money I wasted paying him and asked if I had lost my damn mind.

Shortly after that I was given an assignment in Vietnam. Before shipping off I hired movers to ship furniture home to Ohio and then put her and the kids on an airplane to live with her mother. I was in Vietnam for quite a few months and asked for an extension until it was time for my discharge. I was making good money because I was collecting all kinds of bonus money: combat pay, hazardous duty pay, family separation pay, overseas pay. While I was in Southeast Asia, I never spent a dime. My wife was getting a bi-monthly check for her and the kids, and I sent her some money to make ends meet and then bank the rest.

While I was in Vietnam, I sometimes went out into the bush with Fountain to visit Special Forces camps Dak To and Dak Pek to relate intelligence. In case our pilots had to bail out, they would know where to find the camps, and the Special Forces team would know how and where to retrieve the pilots. I liked Dak Pek best.

A team consisted of twelve Special Forces soldiers: the officer in charge, and a warrant officer second in charge, and then two each of weapons specialists, engineers, medics, communications specialists, and intelligence specialists. These guys went deep into the jungle and befriended the indigenous Montagnard people. We called them Yards for short. They've been in the mountains of Vietnam for centuries, driven there by the Cambodians. Even in 1965 these people still wore loincloths and used spears.

I recall the first time we visited Dak Pek. It was tradition to meet the chief in his hut. Dried rats hung from his ceiling, and he would offer you a piece. You couldn't refuse because it would be an insult. It didn't taste too bad dipped in a sauce that tasted something like soy sauce.

That night they threw a welcome party for Colonel Fountain and me. They played music on gongs while men in ceremonial dress beat a cow with sticks to tenderize the meat. When the cow fell to its knees, the chief slit its throat, filled two small cups with blood and handed it to the colonel and me to drink. After that they butchered and cooked the cow.

In the meantime there was a drinking ceremony. They had ancient crocks—which I bet were worth a fortune—that held about fifty gallons each of *pae na* (rice wine). There were dead flies and all sorts of debris floating on the top. They put the end of a stick about two inches into the crock. You had to drink through the straw—which was an IV tube provided by the medics—without coming up for air until the stick was no longer submerged in the wine.

I was not a drinker but made it through, and everyone clapped and cheered. And the chief placed a copper bracelet around my wrist. Some of the Special Forces guys had multiple bracelets on each arm. Of course you end up stinking drunk.

For their loyalty Uncle Sam armed the Yards so they could protect themselves from the Viet Cong, provided medical care, and fed them. There could be as many as two to three hundred indigenous people in one camp. Food was parachuted in by a C130 aircraft—everything from cows, chickens, and pigs to rice. There was a medical call once a week. The villagers would line up for anything from pregnancy to cuts and abrasions. They also handed out soap and teach them hygiene.

Me in camouflage while in Vietnam

I pulled the duty of supervising the guards a couple of nights from midnight to three in the morning. There would be at least ten Yards lined up and waiting for me to inspect their weapons. After inspection they dispersed to their posts located all around the camp. At dark, all lights and fires are put out. I made my rounds to check on the guards to ensure they were alert. I was informed that a certain Yard guard might be lighting a small fire to give the VC the camp's location. I was told by the captain that if I caught the guard lighting a fire, to blow him away. I had never killed anyone before and was praying that I wouldn't be the one to catch the firelighter.

One night I went on patrol with four Special Forces team members and about twenty Yards. We were walking single file on a narrow trail in the jungle. I was about midway from the point. Suddenly there was a lot of commotion up at the point, and the detail came to a halt. I rushed up to see what was going on, and there was a very large python crossing our path. I did a quick about-face and headed away from the snake, knocking down just about every Yard in my path. By the time I recovered, the Yards had that snake cut up and bagged. It would be that night's meal. Tasted like chicken to me.

I liked working with the team, and I liked the Yards. . I stuck around an extra week after Fountain returned to the base. You had to get home by catching any kind of cargo plane or convoy that moved through Vietnam. It was a pretty long journey of catching several rides since the camps were located close to the Laotian border.

After returning to the airbase, I volunteered for flying back seat with a pilot from another base for forward air control duty, which was designed to ensure that an attack hit the intended target and prevented friendly fire casualties. We flew in an old Cessna with controls front and back. FAC directed airstrikes from tree-top level. I wouldn't exactly call it safe, but the VC was less likely to shoot at you because it would give away their position—at least, that's what I was told.

I was to meet the FAC on the flight line at 0600 hours (6:00 a.m.). and was waiting in the middle of nowhere. The pilot showed up about fifteen minutes late, saying he'd had a rough night in the officer's club. There were no introductions. I immediately jumped into the back seat and strapped in, then the pilot taxied and lined the plane up for takeoff. His charts and maps should have been done the night before or that morning before him taking off from his home base, but he's been out drinking. So once the tower gave permission to take off, the pilot asked me to take off and climb up to six thousand feet and take a northwest heading because he needed to put his mission preparation chart together. He assumed he had a fighter pilot riding along as his second set of eyes.

I took off and climbed up to his prescribed altitude and heading. He then introduced himself as Captain Johns, then asked me what type of fighter I flew. When I told him I wasn't a pilot, he grabbed his stick so hard that he almost put the plane into a roll. He wanted to know how in hell I managed to take off, and I explained how I self-taught myself with the help of the flight simulator boys back at Homestead Air Force Base. But I warned him not to ask me to land, and he assured me he wouldn't.

After we finished calling in the airstrikes, he flew me back to the base. I went into operations where there were a few pilots getting ready to go up. I told them what had happened, and everyone in the tent roared with belly-busting laughter. I remember asking some pilots how they stayed up all night drinking and still went out on combat missions.

They told me: *You have to be drunk or crazy to be a pilot flying in combat.*

We had a list posted on a bulletin board with those of us that wanted to go up and be observers. My name was next on the list. But Colonel Fountain said he needed me with him and told another guy named De Tomasso to switch places with me.

Me in Vietnam in flight suit, G-suit, Mae West life jacket. Side firearm, and parachute slung over my left shoulder, heading for back seat combat mission in F-100 fighter jet

He never returned from that flight.

Nobody ever knew what happened, just that he and the pilot were missing in action. No one knew whether they were alive or prisoners of war. And I never found out. For years I wondered what had happened to him. In 1997 I went to the Vietnam War Memorial in Washington, DC, and found his name. *Robert J De Tomasso, Missing in Action.*

I couldn't help but cry.

BACK TO COLLEGE

After I got discharged in August 1967, my dad picked me up at the airport, and on the way home asked to borrow some money. I loaned him $500 just to get him off my back, knowing I would never see that money again.

The first thing I did was buy a red new 1967 Chevy Impala, paying cash. Then I rented a small house in Martins Ferry and moved in with my wife and kids. Using skills I had learned with my uncle in Cleveland and my dad, I fixed that quaint little house up like it was mine. Then I got a phone call from Dr. Blatnik, who was head of the Physical Education Department and assistant football coach at West Liberty. He asked if I planned on coming back to school, and I said yes. Bo had gotten discharged a few months earlier than me and was already back there finishing up his degree. Dr. Blatnik asked if I could come and meet with him and the football coaches.

I went to see them the following day, and they offered me a full scholarship with everything paid for, including the dorm. I accepted. I reported to preseason football camp and was immediately put in the starting line up ahead of the tight end that had started the last two years. But they all knew that I'd been all-conference prior to my returning. Coach Kavolic was gone; now it was Coach Roe. I stayed on campus during the two weeks of training camp but called home every night. Once the preseason practice was over and classes were about to start, I went home.

It was a Saturday night, and what a surprise. I saw my two children looking out the big picture window. When I tried to open the door, it was locked. I told them to open the door, but they wouldn't. I asked them where their mother was, and they kept looking behind them.

There were no cell phones in 1967, so I went to a nearby payphone, called the house, and a man answered.

I asked, "Who is this?"

He replied, "I'm in here f**** your wife," then hung up.

I called again, and she answered laughing and told me to get lost. Anger quickly replaced disbelief. I threatened to run the car straight through the house. She must have believed me because she called the police. When the officers arrived, they found me hysterical and crying. They knew who I was from my dad's club. They calmed me down and insisted on one of them driving my car to the club. I refused to go there because I was in no mood to hear *I told you so*.

They took me to an old, abandoned steel mill, telling me my wife wasn't worth getting into trouble over, especially after I told them it was the second time. They told me that they patrolled the area, and they'd seen the man's car parked outside my house before. I figured she'd been having an affair while I was in Vietnam.

I got over it pretty quick. I'd probably been over her since that first time in Florida. So, I hired a divorce lawyer, and this time I signed the papers.

###

During my last two years of college, I had it made. I had everything paid for, including a meal ticket, the GI Bill, and a summer job in the steel mill. They gave me an Ohio scholarship, which was worth twice as much as a West Virginia scholarship. I registered; using my new best friend Larry's West Virginia address. (I had met Larry at football camp.) Somehow the registration office didn't coordinate with the finance office. Each semester I received an Ohio scholarship check, and when paying, I got half of the money back. At that time, it was about $2,500—more than enough in 1967 to pay cash for most American cars or

Me going out for a pass reception my senior year in college during homecoming

a down payment on a house. I know that this seems dishonest, but I felt it was payback for what I went through my freshman and sophomore years. I was swimming in cash.

My last two years in school, I dated a couple of White girls by chance. It got pretty serious with the first girl, Bobby, who commuted every day. She tried several times to get me to come home with her to meet the parents, assuring me several times that her parents would just love me. She told me that her dad and mother took in Black high school athletes when they came for the state championships because their house was right by the stadium. I reiterated that it wasn't a good idea but finally gave in and went there to dinner on Christmas Eve. Both parents were very cordial when we were introduced. We had dinner, and then the talk began. Bobby started off by saying how much she cared for me and asked for their blessing. I repeated what she said and added that I would be a good provider should the relationship go further.

The father asked, "If you had to provide for her, how would you do it?"

Before I could get a word out, my girlfriend said, "Daddy, he makes more money than you do now, and he's still in college."

At that time I had the GI Bill, half of my tuition reimbursed to me, was student teaching, and had a full-time steel mill job where I was allowed to sleep after two hours of clerk work.

But her dad answered by saying, "If God meant for two people of different races to be together, he would have made us all the same."

I kept my cool and let him go on. I gave no argument.

The mother said, "Daddy, how can you say that when I'm an

American Indian?"

He told her to shut her mouth and that the conversation was over. After that meeting, my girlfriend was willing to go all out and sacrifice her parents for me. I wasn't quite ready for that commitment, and I didn't want to be the one causing her to be estranged. We dated for a little while longer, then grew apart. I was picked for all-conference in both football and the discus in track and held the conference record for many years.

During my senior year, the Denver Broncos came to the campus and told me I'd be drafted in the tenth round and to stay by the phone. I'm still waiting for the call. Needless to say, I never got drafted.

LIFE AFTER COLLEGE

After graduation the Continental Football League's farm team for the Pittsburgh Steelers, the Wheeling Ironmen, invited me to camp. I also started dating another White girl, Diane, who was a senior at West Liberty State who lived in Wheeling, twelve miles away. During the season I gave her tickets for the family. I picked her up from campus and drove her home. At times her parents were sitting on the front porch when I dropped her off. They were fans of mine, so they waved and said hello, convinced that I was just their daughter's friend.

Me making a key catch with the Wheeling Ironmen, aiding in winning the game

Again, here was another girlfriend insisting that I come to dinner, so we could break the news that we were an item. After several arguments I gave in again. Diane's dad and teenaged brother were excited to have me at the house. After dinner she got straight to the point and revealed our little secret.

Her brother reached across the table and punched Diane in the face.

The dad turned red. "No way! What are my neighbors and friends going to say? No God damn way!"

Her mother had nothing to say and kept out of it. They got no argument from me.

I could never understand how some people could be crazy over Black athletes, wear their jerseys, and fight to get an autograph but be prejudiced at the same time. Go figure.

We continued dating for a little while after that ordeal, and Diane told me some of the threats her father made, like: *If you keep seeing him, we aren't your parents anymore, and you'll have to get out of this house.* He also offered to buy her a new car if she stopped seeing me. I figured it would help my girlfriend out by calling her dad and agreeing with him that Black and White shouldn't be together. It hurt me to do that, but someone had to be the bigger man and take it on the chin. I did it for Diane's sake.

Years later we reconnected, and over dinner she told me she had gotten married shortly after graduation to a guy that the parents and relatives just loved. His degree was in business and finance. A couple of years after their marriage, he swindled her parents, her grandparents, and some of her other relatives out of their life savings. They thought he was investing their money because he gave them fake monthly statements. That marriage didn't last long. Diane married again, but that marriage didn't last long either.

She said with a laugh, "After my two episodes of marriage, you'd be looking pretty good to my dad."

Diane had one teenaged son from her first marriage. He was a really nice boy, and I could sense that his mother raised him without bias. She had told him all about me.

Going back to football, I finished the season with the Ironmen, then they folded. The following season in 1970, the Atlantic Coast Football League held a draft, and I was picked up by the Jersey Tigers, a farm team for the Baltimore Colts. I ended up being a standout and was second in the league for receptions when I broke my leg with four games remaining.

I was out for the rest of the season, so I sought a teaching position at Abraham Clark High School in Roselle, New Jersey, and went to the interview on crutches, with a cast up to my hip. I was hired to teach ninth-grade history and drivers' education. I really liked teaching history since it was my major and gave me the chance to emulate my college professor, Dr. Baney. He was so interesting you didn't want his lectures to end. I wanted to have the same effect on my students. I also wanted to make sure that I left no student behind.

I always got pieces of everything growing up, especially in school. It wasn't a good feeling. But I was smart enough to put enough pieces together to pass my tests. I didn't want my students to feel that way. If I had to crawl on the floor and act as if I were hit by a spear or imitate riding a horse charging into battle or act like a ruler sitting on his throne with arrogance, I would do it. Pretty sure some of my students thought that I was crazy. But at every level I held in education, I was always a sucker for the students, I think because I didn't get any special attention in elementary or high school, and not much attention at home, and I didn't give my own children the attention they needed.

The principal of the high school at that time could see that I had his back. I went above and beyond my job description: you could find me breaking up students' disputes, volunteering for chaperoning at school events, and getting involved in anything school-related. There had just been some racial unrest, and by going beyond and above my duties alongside the head of security, we became friends. As a result of my actions, the principal, the head of security, and I eventually became best of friends while at Abraham Clark—and for years to come. We were like the three musketeers.

Even though I didn't finish the season with the Jersey Tigers due to injury, the New York Giants called me to camp in the summer of 1971. If I didn't make the team, I still had my job teaching in the fall.

Prior to going to Giant's camp, I got married to an elementary school teacher. My wife came from a family of means. Her grandparents owned funeral homes that were handed down to their son, my wife's uncle, who grew the business into three funeral homes. The uncle was interracially married to a lady who owned a Lincoln-Mercury dealership and several apartment buildings in Wilmington, New Jersey. Later, I did maintenance for her and my wife's uncle Arthur.

When I met my wife, she lived in a fourteen-room house that previously was a funeral home that was mortgaged to her mother by her mother's parents. Her mother was a divorced, spoiled lady who had dropped out of several colleges. My wife told me that when she was only twelve years old, she had to pay the bills because her mother couldn't care less about her monthly obligations. Her mother had a good job in Manhattan at Bank of America in the check processing department. When she got paid, she neglected her bills and instead went shopping, usually for designer clothes that she'd wear once, throw them on the floor someplace, and go buy more. My wife had to sometimes steal some cash from her mother to pay the utilities.

Her grandmother took custody of her, and she attended Abraham Clark High School. She was one of the very few Blacks in that town. In ninth grade her guidance counselor recommended that she be placed in special education because she was quiet and underachieving in his view. There was no parent conference, no referral to special services for intervention, no nothing but a note from him. Because she was Black he assumed that her grandparents would go for that BS. Little did he know that he was dealing with an educated family.

I mentioned earlier how my father said to always associate yourself with people who could help you. Her grandparents seemed to surround themselves with people that could help them, who mostly happened to be Jewish. Her grandparents immediately took her out of that school, and she was enrolled in Jersey City Academy, an all-Jewish private school. There she participated in different educational clubs, ranked high in her class, and graduated with honors.

Sometimes all it takes is some heartfelt caring and attention to your students as a teacher, especially if you are in a guidance position. Throughout my career I was one of those caring educators. Today I still have former students, some very successful, thanking me for my attention to them. When I was in high school, I didn't realize I had a guidance counselor. Had that not been the best-kept secret, had there been someone to confide in, I think my earlier years would have taken me in a whole different direction.

After my wife finished at the academy, she went off to attend Savannah State, where she excelled academically and became a cheerleader and homecoming queen. When she graduated from Savanna State, she was hired as an elementary school teacher.

Her mother was very devious. She seemed to be in competition with her own daughter. Her mother knew that my wife's great-uncle was going senile, so she pulled a caper with me as the driver. We picked up the uncle in the Bronx where he lived and drove to downtown Manhattan. He wore shabby clothes with an overcoat and his Pullman porter cap; he'd worked as a train porter all of life and had been retired for several years. According to family lore, he looked so bad that people thought that he was a bum and would hand him money—and he took it.

When we reached downtown, the uncle and my wife's mother went into a bank, came back out, and said nothing to my wife and me. We did this at four different banks. We thought the uncle was just getting some business straightened out. When they were done, we dropped him off at his home and went back to New Jersey. We didn't see her mother for quite some time after that.

Our new house was located in Marlboro, New Jersey, near the state mental institution. One day that uncle called my wife from that all upset and crying.

"Please get me out of here! Your mother tricked me and put me in here. These people are all crazy; I don't want to be here."

We immediately drove to the hospital to find out what was going on. The supervisor said that he was free to go anytime because he'd signed himself in. We came to find out that my mother-in-law tricked the uncle into thinking that the mental institution was a regular hospital, and that's why he signed himself in. He'd been there for at least a month. If he wasn't crazy before, he might have been by the time we got him. We took him home to stay with us and found out the story got even better/worse.

My mother-in-law collected more than $200,000 on those bank stops—which is the equivalent of more than $1 million today. That's how she paid cash for a brand-new house similar to ours a few miles away from us.

My wife called her grandmother and grandfather—the great-uncle's brother—and explained what their daughter had done. Dishonesty was par for the course, but it was on a much larger scale this time. They couldn't bring themselves to put their own daughter in jail, so they let her keep the house but made her return the remainder of the money.

The great-uncle was going senile, and it was getting difficult for us to care for him. We both had to work, so my wife would make his breakfast and lunch and label them so he would know which to eat first. But he got continually worse and started wandering. Sometimes my wife had to leave work to go get him in a town miles away from where we lived. The police held him until she got there.

We conferred with my wife's grandmother about what to do with him. Unfortunately, he ended up back in the mental institution, but in a different department that dealt with dementia. We visited often, and he seemed to make new friends and liked where he was. I don't believe that my wife and her mother had too much to do with each other after that.

While in the Giant's camp, I was reassured by one of the coaches that I would make the team. I was told that they planned to keep two tight ends: me and Bob Tucker, who had led the Atlantic Coast Football League in receptions in 1968 and 1969 for the Pottstown Firebirds.

I remember press day: former NY Giant legend Y. A. Tittle, a multitude of press, and Howard Cosell were present. A few days later Coach Webster promised the weekend off, and many of the veterans flew their families in. In the meantime, we had an inter-squad game, and Coach Webster changed his mind about the weekend off because he was upset with how we played. He made us practice that Saturday with shoulder pads and helmets. Many players were upset and were going nearly full speed. Coach kept yelling to cut it out and warning that he might get rid of someone if the hard hitting persisted.

I believe that I was set up on purpose because Fran Tarkington kept throwing the ball to me over and over across the middle. It was supposed to be a two-hand touch. Matt Heseltine, middle linebacker, kept catching me off guard and giving me the shoulder pretty hard. I said to myself that the next time he did it, I'd be ready for him. So I braced after I caught the ball, and Hazeltine went into a crouch as if he were going to tackle me. Somehow my legs got tangled with Hazeltine's. He was lying on the ground, screaming, and holding his already bum knee. I truly believed that he was faking. Before I knew it, Webster threw his hat on the ground, yelling, "I told you guys to stop f****** around!"

The following day I was called into the general manager's office and was cut. He said that they liked the way I played and caught the ball, but he was putting me on waivers. He even offered to call the Philadelphia Eagles for me because they were looking for a tight end. My stupid pride reared its head, and I said no because I had put all my eggs in one basket with the Giants, and I didn't want to take the chance of getting cut again.

As I was driving down the NJ turnpike, greatly disappointed and listening to the radio, Howard Cosell came on the air and said, "Isn't it strange that the Giants let Ken Holmes go?"

I also heard him say the same thing on TV that evening. I didn't know how to face all my students. I'd never been cut from any team before. Had I been single without a new mortgage and marriage, I would have kept trying until I made a team. But my wife wasn't too happy about me playing anyhow.

In the news I saw that the Giants signed old washed-up Dick Kotite as a second tight end. Rumor had it that Webster and Kotite were old drinking buddies. Seems like who you know may also play a part in making an NFL team. I realize that you have to be pretty good to get there, but if your father played, it doesn't hurt either. Webster liked to fraternize with the older players. After Kotite retired from playing, he became the head coach of the Philadelphia Eagles. Go figure.

I came to terms with myself that my football days were over; instead, I settled for teaching and doing home improvement. After returning home from the NY Giants camp in late August, I teamed up with a coworker and friend named Charles Chrebet. We painted houses and took on just about any other job that came our way. One job was painting a funeral home that belonged to my wife's uncle. We took time out for lunch and used an embalming table in the morgue to sit on while eating. We noticed a small wooden box on the table and asked an employee of the funeral home named Sam what was in the box.

"A baby," he said and walked out of the room.

Charlie and I both said *no way!* Of course we had to look because Sam had to be putting us on. So we gingerly opened the box, then screamed like little children. There was definitely a baby in that box.

I worked with Charlie for a few summers. After he quit moonlighting I continued painting and doing general contracting on a small scale. And after teaching at the high school for a couple of years, I became an assistant coach for football and track coaching. The job paid peanuts and took up a lot of my time, but there were kids involved. In addition to coaching after school and doing general contracting, I was also remodeling our home, adding another masonry fireplace, installing an in-ground swimming pool, and building a waterfall in the backyard.

I was a workaholic and was determined not to ever do without. I wanted a piece of the good life even without playing professional football. I was so into what I wanted that for most of my marriage I'd had very little consideration for what my wife might want. I rarely saw her even when home because I'd often work until the wee hours in the morning. Like father, like son.

When coaching I brought students home with parental permission to stay the weekend, feeding them, swimming with them, and giving them little jobs so they could have some pocket change. It wasn't because all of them were poor; it was that they needed a little empathy or attention. Sometimes I invited the entire football team to the house for a cookout and swimming. My wife was a saint to put up with it all.

Now don't get me wrong; there were arguments at times. And her grandmother would urge her to go on vacation and enjoy herself.

"Don't be like me; we're sitting on all this money, and I've never been any place, so go every time you get a chance."

But my wife was just like her grandmother while married to me. I refused several times to go on vacation with her; my excuse was I had already seen the world and had no interest. This went on several summers during our marriage. Then on our seventh anniversary she surprised me with tickets for a three-week tour of Europe. I couldn't even fathom something like that and said I wasn't going. Since the vacation for two was already paid for, she took her aunt. But I broke her heart that time. I don't know if it was like father, like son or just plain stupidity on my part.

When she returned from vacation, our relationship began to sour. I take all the blame because I still could have warmed up to her, but I didn't know how. Even today most of my siblings don't hug and kiss each other, I guess because we never saw that kind of affectionate behavior from our parents or relatives. And I didn't show my wife the affection she needed either. So the best thing that ever happened to me drifted away. A few months later we agreed to an amicable split. She didn't want anything from me or from the house. She said she hated the house because it was all about me, so I could have it. Her family attorney drew up the divorce papers. There was no monetary consideration, but the terms stipulated that after two years, we'd have the house appraised, and I would have to pay her half of the equity if I continued living in there. If I couldn't afford to, we'd sell the house, and she would get half the proceeds. Knowing her, that part wasn't her idea but the attorney's.

You'd think that after the split, I would have learned my lesson. Instead I started working more than ever. I guess working was my comfort zone that gave me peace of mind, plus I now had to survive on one salary.

AFTER THE SECOND MARRIAGE

Within a year or so after our divorce, my ex-wife lost her grandmother, grandfather, and great uncle. While she was in all their wills, I was left to pay the mortgage, two car payments, and the monthly bills on a single income. After the two years were up, I didn't have the means to give her half of the equity and sold the house. But there wasn't a lot of equity in it since the house was only seven years old.

After the house was sold, the equity check went straight to her attorney. Shortly after that we met in her lawyer's office to receive our shares of the sale. Her lawyer handed us our checks. She signed hers then slid it to me across the table. Her attorney and I were both taken aback. As we walked out of the office together, I asked why she had me sell the house and then give me her share.

"I hate that house and wanted you out of there too."

I didn't know whether to cry or get mad. In the end I figured I had that coming. I would have to live in an apartment until I got back on my feet.

Our meeting with the attorney took place shortly before my birthday. I came home from moonlighting one evening and found a new 1978 Lincoln Continental Mark IV in my assigned parking space. There was a huge ribbon on the roof and a birthday card attached. I was a little upset at first that someone had the nerve to park in my space—and in my dream car no less. Then I saw the card had my name on it in big, bold letters. It was a gift from my wife.

Shortly after that her family gave me a deed to a three-family brownstone in the Bronx close to Yankee Stadium. My wife's great-uncle bequeathed the house to her and his nephew (his brother's son who owned the funeral homes). Instead of selling it, they gave it to me since I knew how to maintain it. She said that she had received quite a nice inheritance and had we still been married, I would have been a part of it, so the house was the least that she could do for me.

Who does that? I really did let the best thing that ever happened to me get away, all for stupid pride.

The house they gifted me was occupied by three tenants, including the super, whose rent was very low. Her great-uncle had been deceased for over a year, and only the super had put aside money for rent. The other tenants apparently thought they could live there for free since the owner had died. They hadn't paid rent for thirteen months—and still weren't. I tried to collect the back rent but had no luck.

So I filed an eviction notice, and it took about six months to get a court hearing. At first the judge jumped down my throat, asking me how I let the nonpayment go so long. Once I explained that I had inherited the situation, he understood and asked the two delinquent tenants if they any money on them. One had $700 and the other $1300. The judge had them hand the money to me directly and said if they weren't current on all the back rent in five days, they and their belongings would be on the street.

Those tenants left, leaving just the super. In my estimation, the building was pretty far gone. Some of the exterior was stone, but the outside wood and gutters needed repair. I also didn't want to take a chance on the infrastructure. I knew that the house wouldn't sell for much, so I offered to sell it to the super for $30,000—why not give someone else a break? The super was pretty handy and could fix it up and then the tenants would take care of his expenses.

The super tried to get a mortgage loan from several banks and was turned down by them all. He and his wife's combined income would qualify with just about any bank had they been White. But they were Black. So I financed him myself with a seven-year mortgage with 3 percent interest and a balloon payment of $7,000 at the end of the seven years. He paid me $5,000 down, and I received monthly payments of $238.

I would save that money, the money from the equity from my house, and what I earned moonlighting because I wanted a big house on a sizable piece of land in Somerset County, New Jersey, an upscale area with many prestigious people and equally upscale property values. The problem was, I had champagne tastes with beer money. But I was *determined*.

UPWARD BOUND

In the interim of my department chairman and moonlighting days, I contacted Burgdorff Realty, a Jewish realtor that had one of their offices located in Somerset County. My agent, Mr. Goldman, was going to help me find my dream property. Once or twice a week, he'd show me properties, but they were either too expensive, too hilly, or not to my liking for whatever reason. But the main obstacle was money, and after a while I didn't hear from Goldman for a few months. I thought he'd given up on me because of my finances.

Then out of nowhere, Goldman called me and said that he might have something I'd be interested in if I had an imagination. He also said that if I were to purchase the property, located in Bridgewater, New Jersey, I'd likely go through hell in that area because of what I looked like—meaning, being Black—but urged me not to let anyone discourage me because the land could become very profitable in the future if I could persevere.

Perseverance was my name.

The property was part of a probate, and the will couldn't be settled until it was sold. The heirs were all young people who couldn't care less about the property or even going to see it. As far as they were concerned, it was worth peanuts compared to what they were going to receive. They thought it was just a piece of wasteland that their grandfather, who owned Franklin Contracting Company, left them along with megabucks.

The land was forty-eight acres with big craters all over the place from the contracting company extracting gravel to use as bedding to build US

Rte. 22, and huge dirt hills were piled on two sides of the property. The owner had also allowed the Somerset County Police Department to set up a firing range on the land. Bordering the property was the north branch of the Raritan River, which was a popular fishing spot.

I thought *I'll have my own private river!*

I did have a big imagination and really wanted this piece of wasteland. I could see far beyond craters and junk cars. Goldman told me I had an advantage to grab this property because it wasn't on the market yet and should make an offer of $90,000. That was way out of my league; the most I could scrape would be about $60,000, which was nothing to spit at in the seventies.

Goldman knew how badly I wanted that dream property. He said he had told his boss, Mrs. Burgdorff, about me, that I was hard-working, taking flying lessons, teaching, and very ambitious. So when I told him that I'd be $30,000 short, he thought Mrs. Burgdorff might be able to help.

The next day Goldman called and asked if I could come in that afternoon to meet with Mrs. Burgdorff. When I arrived at her office, she was wearing jodhpurs and riding boots. She was pretty, probably in her fifties, and very refined. She asked me to excuse her appearance; I assured her it was no problem. I enjoyed riding too. That led to a discussion about how as a kid in rural Ohio, I learned to ride Western on farmer's horses, but I now rode English as well since befriending a lawyer who lived in Harding Township, an upscale part of Morris County, New Jersey.

She smiled. "I like you already. You remind me of my son. I understand that you're taking flying lessons. My son flies too. You and he are both ambitious."

She said she would loan me the $30,000. When she added, "What do you say to three percent?" her company lawyer, who had been sitting quietly in the corner, loudly cleared his throat.

She asked her attorney what he thought would be fair, and of course

Me with some of my students, picking out spots to pitch tents while camping on my property. There were fifty students in attendance.

he suggested a ridiculous percentage rate. She said no way and offered a six-year, five percent loan with a $7,000 balloon payment at the end.

I agreed without even thinking how I'd pull it off. But at that moment all that mattered was I now owned almost fifty acres in Somerset County with a river boundary, complete privacy, a 1,100-foot-long, fifty-foot-wide driveway that led into the property. And the land was surrounded by a fairy large new development.

The first thing I did was purchase an old Caterpillar bulldozer to clear out the abandoned cars and trucks and clear as much as I could without a permit. I would not build a house there until six years later, after I paid off the mortgage in 1984, but prior to that I used the property as camping grounds for my physical education program.

Shortly after the property closed, I went to the planning office to get a copy of my site map, which depicts elevations and boundaries. When I walked up to the large reception counter, everyone stopped working, I'm sure without realizing it. I felt like I usually did most of the time when walking into places where I was the only Black person. You feel like you are a Martian.

When I requested a copy of lot 46, block 152, the clerk asked, "Why would you want to see that?"

Not the answer I wanted to hear because I knew where this was going to go. To start I played dumb.

"Isn't this information public?" (It is.)

But he went on and on until I finally revealed that the property was mine. He said to his knowledge, no it wasn't.

Wow.

Trying hard to keep my cool, I whipped out the paperwork. Now he and another gentleman were at the counter asking me how exactly I bought the property and other demeaning questions. I gave them my go-to sarcastic answer over the years whenever a White person asked how I afforded some of the cars I had owned.

"I saved up all of my welfare checks."

I hated doing it, but they brought the uppity out of me—that's the word White folks used for Black people when they didn't know their place. All of the onlookers quickly turned away except for one gentleman who thought my comment funny and laughed. The two clerks informed me that my plot was a wasteland, and I had wasted my money.

Their lack of enthusiasm got the best of me, and I took my map and left the building feeling really low, believing who would know about the property than people working in that office. But then I remembered what Mr. Goldman said about my determination, and I shrugged off the clerks' lack of support or enthusiasm.

The following day I received a phone call from a man who introduced himself as Bob Trucill. He was the guy who had laughed at my welfare comment. He was a former city engineer who was starting his own business.

"Don't let those idiots discourage you," he told me, then offered to help me with that property and gave me his address and phone number. That gave me a big boost.

I went to see him a few days later with a set of house plans. He took my blueprints and said that he would take it from there and referred me to an attorney, Ron Ferb. He told me I would definitely need him to go before the planning board once the site plan was finished. By now word leaked out from the code office that a Black man owned a large parcel in Bridgewater. I didn't even ask what the engineering fees would be.

I'd often go to the property just to look around and stick my chest out as if I were a land baron, taking in the scenery and picturing in my mind what I wanted the finished product to look like. The property would be a hunter's dream. It had white-tailed deer running all over, wild turkeys, coyotes, red fox, Canadian geese, and a private river to fish.

One afternoon I found a couple of dozen policemen at the firing range that was on the property. When I got out of my truck, one policeman shouted at me.

"Get back in your vehicle and go back where you came from!"

I forced a smile and asked who was in charge. A lieutenant stepped forward.

"I am. What can I do for you?"

I introduced myself and told him that I owned the property.

"I guess you're going to throw us out of here because of the way you were greeted a minute ago."

"The thought crossed my mind."

I told him they could stay and that I'd give them ample notice before construction on the house started, which would be where the firing range currently was. The officer thanked me and apologized.

Shortly after that the police moved out, and I made a makeshift fence out of thick cable and pieces of an old telephone pole and placed it at the entrance of the property on Meadow Road. Several times when I arrived at the property, I'd find the *nigger* and *porch monkey* spray-painted on several trees and on the dirt driveway. It was ongoing and started getting serious when I found my bulldozer had been set on fire. Nearby was a sign with *nigger stay away* written on it.

But it's pretty hard to burn an iron machine. I replaced all electric cables and rubber hydraulic hoses, and it ran like new again.

Bit by bit I cleared and cleaned the property. Sometimes I gave weekend jobs to some senior students. The kids would drag brush and tree branches and stack tree logs after I cut the trees down. I never told my students—or anyone else for that matter—about my racial woes at the property.

One Friday while at school, a couple of senior boys said they had a few students who wanted to volunteer to help me on the property. I had no problem with that, and on the following morning an entourage of students, both girls and boys, showed up to help. It was a bit chilly out, so we built a controlled campfire. As we were all working, two police cars came speeding down my driveway, then stopped near the fire where some girls were standing.

The rest of the students were with me on top of a hill cutting trees. When I saw the police cars, I came down the hill and asked if I could help them. They asked me if I was in charge. I replied yes.

"Who's your boss?"

"Me."

One policeman said, "Don't get smart."

"I'm not getting smart. I am my own boss, and I own this property."

"*You* own this property?"

Again I said yes. My twelve White students got to see for themselves how I was treated as a Black man.

Then one of the officers asked, "Whereabouts is the fire that we were called here for?"

The students all pointed at our small fire with grins on their faces as if to say: *You are idiots for treating Mr. Holmes this way.*

At that moment two fire trucks with sirens blasting came down the driveway. The firemen jumped out and asked where the fire was. Again, all the students pointed to our small campfire.

The policemen left immediately. The head fireman apologized and explained they had to put out the fire.

"But after we leave, what we don't know, we don't care about."

From that time until a few years later, I'd constantly get surprise visits from township officials, from code inspectors to the dog catcher based on anonymous complaints and accusations. I had no idea who the culprit was making the calls.

There was one student that I was especially fond of, Martin Limbeck, who was on a foreign exchange program from Germany. As physical education chairman, I'd go to the different phys ed classes and noticed a tall, handsome blonde student seemed to be alone all the time while in his assigned class. After observing this kid for a few days, I picked the opportune time to lambast all juniors and seniors in that particular class.

Attendance was taken in the gymnasium for about 120 students each period. I interrupted the teachers taking attendance.

"I can't believe that none of you were compassionate enough to welcome Martin to the school, show him, around and befriend him. What's wrong with all of you? This kid is thousands of miles away from home on his own in a completely strange country. If any of you were in his situation, you'd be crying for your mothers. You all should be ashamed."

Not long after that, Martin started to get some new friends, including Eric Struck.

A day later or so, I pulled Martin to the side to chat with him to see how he was doing. He then told me that his host family was always arguing with one another, and the husband didn't try to hide the fact that he didn't care for Martin. What a thing to do to a kid so far away from home. Why in the hell would he even sign up for the program and treat a kid that way.

The Struck family kindly took Martin in. And if the Strucks hadn't, I would have gladly taken him in myself. I took Martin under my wing, and that made both Martin and me happy. I gave Martin a job every now and then helping me on the property. While working, Martin told me that he would be a rich man one day, and I would be proud of him. I took him fishing on the property and horseback riding at a friend's farm. Martin was included in all the extracurricular school activities, including a weekend ski trip to Canada with me and forty or so of his classmates.

Martin's parents came to the United States for his graduation, and I invited them to stay with me, and they did. They stayed several days, and we took a couple of day trips, played tennis, and toured part of New York City. After he returned to Germany, Martin often called to tell me how he was doing and always said he would be a wealthy man one day.

We eventually lost track of each other because I went off the grid, so to speak, for thirty years until we found each other some thirty years later in 2020. And he had done exactly what he said he would; he is a wealthy and successful man.

I finally got an audience with the planning board, and it was my responsibility to notify all neighbors within so many feet of the property by certified mail. When my engineer Bob, my attorney Ron, and I arrived at the meeting, it was standing room only. The mayor was my biggest adversary, as if he'd already promised the town that he would make sure I would never build a house and move there. After his ranting and calling my property a lake with a moat, the meeting was open to the public.

There were so many ignorant questions and statements it made me want to scream, but I let the people I was paying take care of my business. My engineer had all of his ducks in order with elevations, soil impacts, setbacks, etc. My attorney was there to quell any nonsense the board might try. The board had no choice but to grant me a building permit regardless of the mayor's and the public's disdain. After the meeting adjourned, two ladies approached and welcomed me to the neighborhood. That was the beginning of my way upwards but not without obstacles on the way.

About a year or so after the false alarm fire, I started building my dream home in 1984. My dad always said, don't let unprofessional mess your car or your house. Again, I didn't listen to my dad because he was wrong in just about everything he said, so I chose the opposite. The house was designed as a five thousand square foot, modern cedar siding house with multiple roofs, many skylights, sliding doors, and all windows with tinted glass. I guess growing up in an 1,800 square foot house in Rayland with ten children gave me a space complex.

I did much of the construction myself but need to subcontract out the roof framing. I ended up hiring a Black crew, figuring I'd give business to one of my people. When the all-Black crew showed up, they were wearing fedoras like Indiana jones, old dress pants instead of coveralls, and old dress shoes instead of work shoes. This kind of scared me, but you can't always judge a book by looking at the cover. I showed them where all the materials were and left because I was converting a barn into an apartment in another town.

I stopped by the property a couple of days later, and nobody was at the worksite even though their cars were there. I found them at the river, fishing. They went back to work and said they would be finished in a couple of days for sure. So I arranged for the inspector to come out in three days so I could get the next bank payment for flooring and sheathing.

They finished up just in time for the building inspector. After the crew packed up and left, I looked at the completed roof framing. Something didn't look right to me. I couldn't see how the different roofs were going to breathe. I called the contractor that evening, and he reassured me that the roofs were framed correctly.

When the inspector showed up the next morning, he immediately started shaking his head. "This entire roof has to come off because it will rot in about ten years because it won't be able to breathe."

I never tried to recoup my loss because I knew it would be futile. So I chalked it up as my fault.

It was the second time that I was flimflammed by my own people. When I first got into home improvement, I needed a pickup truck but didn't have the money for a new one. I knew a guy who knew a guy who owned a used car dealership. I should have walked away; The place was a dump.

The dealer had an old pickup truck but ran okay on the test drive. I paid him $800 cash and drove it home. By the time I arrived home, the truck was smoking, and then it quit running completely. I was furious. I called to complain, and it took a week for a tow truck to retrieve the truck. I really needed that truck, so I called the following day to see what the problem was. He told me that he was working on it.

I asked the guy who had recommended him to make sure the dealer put a rush on it. He agreed. When he got to the lot, the truck was sitting far off in a corner. I called again raising hell, and the dealer said that the truck would be ready in two days, and he would call me when finished. I've yet to get that call.

My friend Larry and I made the long drive to retrieve the truck, and when we arrived, the truck was gone. I asked the dealer where it was, and he said that he sold it. I have no words for the way I responded. How could he sell my truck without me signing over the title? Complete silence. I had him by his collar and threatening to kick his ass.

He said, "I know you will and can."

At a loss for words, I unhanded him. I asked him if he had my money. He said that he didn't have it at present, but he would mail it to me. We got in the car and went home. I've yet to receive my money. A few months later, I visited the friend of the dealer, who took me by the dealer's home. It was a mansion that took up a whole corner block.

I had been taken really good. And now it had happened again with my roof framing. I called my engineer, who said I should have called him in the first place. He knew some guys could correct the problem.

The following day the Caccavelli brothers showed up. They were able to save some of the lumber after dismantling the framed structure; the rest I had to repurchase. Two days later we were on the job together, tearing down and reconstructing. I learned a lot. Show me how once, and

I'll take it to the bank later.

When we completed the framing, I requested another inspection. The brothers knew the inspector well, so they were surprised when one of the brothers saw him using a credit card to measure gaps in the joints, looking for a reason to fail the work.

He bellowed at the inspector, "Get that shit out of here. You never pulled that shit on any of the houses we've built. Don't start that bullshit here just because it's Mr. Holmes's house."

The inspector put the card back in his pocket, stamped his approval, and left the site.

Pictures of front, back and side of the house that the Caccavelli brothers helped me build.

After that I hired the Caccavelli brothers to help finish the entire house—framing, masonry, sheathing, and siding. They were general contractors, so they helped me with recommending plumbers, electricians, sheet rockers, etc. Working alongside the Caccavelli brothers, we became friends and would also do some joint construction over the years.

As chairman of physical education, driver education, and health, I had one of the best, most innovative physical education programs in the state, which was called Lifetime Sports. Students were free to choose three activities for each marking period, which included everything from the usual basketball and soccer to horseback riding and snow skiing.

I implemented a battle of the classes, with every student from grade seven through twelve competing. It was an all-day event at the football stadium. There were concession stands sponsored by different classes as fund raisers, a food truck, and a local deli across the street. Every teacher was assigned to scorekeeping, refereeing, or crowd control. The teachers were fed a catered picnic pro bono by me to ensure that they would be there for the entire day. The program gave every student, regardless of athletic ability, a chance to compete.

I also came up with a "superstars" program for grades nine through twelve, which pitted the sixty best athletes in the school against one another in a competition that took place once a year on a course that included wall climbing, tunnels, hurdles, rope climbing, jumping over water, a sprint to the finish line, and a finally of tug of war with all sixty students with water in the center.

Lastly, as chairman I implemented a union called the Supervisors Association. It was a struggle with the Board of Education, but I prevailed. I've never settled for the status quo in my life.

By that time in my career, I had given up coaching. During the three years when I was head football coach, we were conference champs once.

And during my ten years as the head track coach, we were conference champs twice and runners-up for the other eight years.

For all the compassion and concern I had as a teacher and coach, I'm almost ashamed to admit that I gave little attention to

Me as head football coach, giving a play to the quarterback, with assistant coach Louis Grasso looking on.

my own two children throughout their school years. I never attended either one of their graduations or any of my son's basketball games. I guess you could say like father, like son in that aspect. From the time I left Ohio in 1970 to the present, my first wife has tried to turn my children against me as if I was the culprit. To my knowledge my children still don't know their mother and I divorced because of her infidelity. Heaven only knows how many times I wanted to tell them.

Having a two-timing wife hurt me so much, I guess I took my resentment out on the children without realizing it. Even though I had very little contact with my children beyond my control, I still kept my obligations. And while I spent very little time with my children during Christmas and birthdays, there wasn't one Christmas or birthday that I didn't send a gift and tell them that I loved them. Then when they became teenagers, they'd answer the phone, and we'd be able to talk until their mother or stepfathers would listen in, discover it was me on the line, and make them hang up.

So I was shocked that she let my daughter come to visit me after her graduation. She spent a week with me. I lived in an apartment at that time. I took her to meet my friends and took her horseback riding for the first time. I asked what she wanted for graduation, and she said a car—she went for the gusto. A couple of weeks later I bought her a car, drove it to her, and flew back to New Jersey.

Shortly after that my daughter developed schizophrenia at age eighteen. That knocked me for a loop. I asked God how this could happen. I did research and found that with the proper medication she could live close to a normal life. But when she turned forty, she developed Parkinson's disease.

My son graduated with a degree in business from the same college I attended, West Liberty University. By that time I was living in my newly built home, and he showed up unannounced. He was living in upstate New York, working as a sales manager for a family that owned multiple dealerships. He told me he could see I wasn't the terrible person his mother always preached. I apologized to him for my behavior over the years, explaining that I let his mother come between me and my children.

We have been as close as possible since then.

ENEMIES WITHIN MY DAY JOB

In 1986 I started interviewing for vice principal at my school and was bypassed several times when my best friend was the principal. Go figure. I assumed it was because I'd been labeled a troublemaker by forcing the chairman union on the Board of Education. After asking the superintendent of schools and the president of the Board of Education a couple of times why I get passed by so often, they both told me, "The principal didn't want you."

What a slap in the face. Forget about him being my best friend, my programs contributed to good student discipline and harmony among the entire student body, and yet my friend was against me. Some friend. After finding this shocking news out, I approached my so-called friend, who was White by the way.

At first he played dumb, then asked for my forgiveness and had the gall to say, "I was afraid you were going to take my job."

I told him that we were finished as friends, but I would continue doing my job just as I always had. A couple of years later, he was removed from the principalship for being ineffective. You would think that meant he'd be demoted, but instead he was placed in the district's best middle school and from there was promoted to superintendent of schools. I witnessed the same thing happen with the principal before him.

When will that happen in the Black world? A Black man replaced my former friend as principal. He didn't care for me either since I was very popular with the student body and the staff. I was passed over a couple of times by him also. In 1992 he finally chose me as vice-principal against his will; I was told the board as a whole insisted that I be one of his vice principals.

As a vice-principal I received a decent raise, and that coupled with my home improvement business, allowed me to perform more improvements to the property and play the stock market. I contracted a heavy equipment company to clear a few acres for pastures. Whatever their giant machines didn't complete, I would work sunup to sundown myself with some former students I hired to cut brush and small trees. My helpers would get lunch breaks, but I would keep working straight through. Even after my helpers went home for the day, I'd continue working. They all said I was crazy. But I was and still am a workaholic. Some of my former students said that when they started dragging ass about three o'clock, I had a smile on my face while working.

I remember hiring one former student, who showed up his first day wearing a brand-new pair of work boots. He worked alongside me all day, even after I told him to take a lunch break. I figured that he was trying to show me, his old football coach, that he could keep up. At the end of the day, he left his work boots at the house and said he would see me the next morning bright and early. He never came back.

A couple of months later, I ran into him at a grocery store and told him that I still had his work boots. While handing him the money he earned for working that day, I asked what had happened.

He said, "You keep your damn money and the damn boots."

I hired the contracting company to level off a large mound of dirt with a huge Caterpillar D-8. That leveled land combined with an acre of flat land gave me an additional two-acre building lot. That flattened piece of land on the front edge of the property would bring me a considerable sum of money without being approved for a subdivision by the planning board.

After I finished clearing all of the future pastures, I befriended a local farmer, Pete, who raised Hereford cattle and hired him to plow my new fields and seed them. The hard and expensive part was fencing the pastures, and it took quite a few dawn-to-dusk days to finish. Pete also got me started with raising my own cattle and sold me my first horse. I named the property Cedar Stone Farm because of all the cedar trees on the property and the gravel. I learned a lot from Pete about animal farming and met other farmers through him. All of the farmers seemed to have a pact to help each other. Sometimes the cattle or horses would break fences and mingle with other cattle. That was to be expected and was no big deal.

Pete also hauled cattle. I would sometimes ride along with him, and we would go to farms belonging to people like future New Jersey Governor Christine Todd Whitman and Malcolm Forbes to haul their cattle to the market or to auctions. King Husain of Jordan owned a fifty-acre vacation farm in the area. By hanging out with Pete, I would eventually get to know many of the local dignitaries, especially Governor Whitman, and become friends. As my dad always said, surround yourself with people who can help you."

The first auction I went to with Pete had prized Hereford bulls worth $20,000 to $50,000 or more—each. Pete told me not to move a muscle—don't wink, don't scratch, don't adjust my cap—so they didn't think I was bidding. Mr. Forbes would attend the auctions. He raised exotic cattle and livestock, and I believe that sheep were his favorite hobby. I passed by his farm many times and would see him in rubber, knee-high boots attending his sheep. He and his wife might be filthy rich, but they appeared to be everyday people.

My gentleman's farm did not turn a profit because I had four horses: an Arabian, a quarter horse, a thoroughbred, and an Andalusia. Owning horses is expensive between veterinarian visits, food, a farrier every two months to groom the hooves, etc. I would get some of the money back I spent on the farm—although nowhere near enough to break even—by having two head of cattle slaughtered yearly, dressed, packaged into several different cuts, and labeled just like a supermarket. I would sell

Some of my horses

eight quarters—120 to 135 pounds each—to my teaching staff at a price they couldn't refuse.

The next step was attempting to subdivide the land. I did a refinance on the property, and the owner of the mortgage company said he would love to move his family to Bridgewater and asked me if I would be willing to subdivide a piece of land. In my area prime land was selling for about $250,000 per acre, and an acre was required to build a house. I invited him over and showed him the areas where a possible subdivision could occur, which was a few hundred yards from my house. Even though I had forty-eight acres, most of the land was in a flood plain, where water has to flow freely in case the river floods. It can be used for pasture and recreational use but not construction. Some of it was wetland that I turned into a beautiful pond.

The mortgage company owner loved the parcel I showed him because it was secluded with a possible hidden driveway. We came to an agreement on price pending planning board approval. I hired my friend Bob, the engineer, to draw up the plans. While he was at it I had him draw up plans for two subdivisions, which were private enough that potential homeowners wouldn't even be able to see each other. I also warned my attorney to prepare for another whirlwind with the town and the mayor. I got my appointment with the planning board and notified the neighbors via certified mail as required.

The meeting was standing room only. The mayor did his expected song and dance, the board members threw in all kinds of shit, and my attorney had to explicate and make sure no curves were thrown. The community added the usual racial innuendos and non-related remarks. The opposition was so fierce that the board made the subdivision pending for a couple of weeks, requiring a few more lines and setbacks to be drawn. I was so offended by the public; I had to remind them that these subdivisions wouldn't be anywhere near their houses, and they wouldn't be able to see the new homes. I also assured them there wouldn't be any low-income housing built.

"These will be $1 million homes—as is mine. I don't see any million-dollar houses, so my homes and the homes to be built will definitely bring up the neighborhood property values."

There was total silence. I just knew that most of the people in that room were dying to drive up to my house to see how I lived.

The meeting adjourned, and two weeks later very few people showed up, which was probably a relief for the planning board, and they granted the subdivision. Both lots were sold: one to the mortgage company owner—who built a $2 million home—and the other to a friend of his, whose house was worth $1.5 million.

Becoming friends with my new neighbor who owned the mortgage company led me into the White world. At times I would need cash for investment projects. Whether it was $150,000, $175,000, or $250,000, I would get it with just a phone call. This happened in the '90s. How can people say there's no such thing as White privilege?

Here is an honest to God story that happened to a Black friend of mine in June 2020. My friend is a multi-millionaire. He owns several condos and homes in a number of states, including a $780,000 lake home in Georgia. His young grandson wanted to buy a jet ski and berth it at his grandfather's dock that has a double lift, one for my friend's boat and the other for a jet ski. They went to the local credit union in that upscale town to give some commerce where he has his home. The jet ski cost $18,000, and the grandson had $5,000 for the down payment. After the application was completed, the loan was turned down for not having good enough credit. My friend said he would cosign and filled out the application. They ran his credit, which showed he had more than enough assets. The loan officer took the application to the manager. She came back and said they needed two years of income statements from his last place of employment.

He said that he had to laugh to keep from crying and cursing. The loan officer was highly apologetic and embarrassed since she was Black and the only Black employee. My friend walked out smiling and gave his grandson the extra $13,000. The day after, he received a phone call with an apology telling him that his grandson didn't need a co-signature.

"He can come and get his money."

Apparently, the actual bank manager made that phone call. But you can imagine what my friend said about that phone call. So yes, this behavior still goes on.

In the meantime, in 1993 I applied for the principalship while my former friend was still the superintendent of schools and was bypassed again. I wondered if he had anything to do with it—of course he did. They hired a Black man named Dr. Bostic from East Orange, New Jersey, who got the position through nepotism; an assistant superintendent was from the same area.

Dr. Bostic had a great gift of gab and turned the procedures and curriculum upside-down with no explanation of how to implement his new directives. He expected his staff to come up with all the answers. I don't know what it was, but this man had no use for me, and I didn't even know him. I'm guessing all these people that were chosen over me were told that I had the favor of the staff and students, and I guess that gave them a complex. But you would think you'd want me on your team. Go figure.

Teachers and department chairs continually complained about how inept he was, and I'm sure news was traveling to the board of education. Dr. Bostic would try to belittle me in the presence of the staff and students. He would see paper on the hallway floor and tell me to pick it up.

That would be one of his biggest mistakes because my reply would be, "I am not a custodian," and the students would laugh.

He also said it was my job to make sure the students dressed properly, whatever that was supposed to mean. He got on me so much that I told him to get off my *** in the presence of staff members, and he wrote me up. I rebutted by recounting all the belittling. Now the gloves were off. I told him I had been there too long, and he couldn't make things so uncomfortable that I'd resign. I also told him I would see that he left before me.

I drew up a petition that all the vice principals and department chairs signed. I attached their complaints to the petition and submitted it to the superintendent—my former friend—and cc'd the board of education, requesting an audience with all parties involved. We had a meeting with the board of education and superintendent, with everyone presenting their complaints aloud. Dr. Bostic was not invited to this meeting, but he showed up regardless, and you could see him pacing back and forth out in the hallway. He was terminated that night. I did not apply for the position for obvious reasons. The board chose a Black lady who was the head of guidance at the high school to replace him; she was somehow related to the new Black superintendent.

I finished that school year and the following year as vice principal. Then in 1995 I asked for a transfer to Leonard V. Moore Middle School to assist a lady who had been the department chairman of mathematics at the high school and was now the middle school principal. I thought it better being with her instead of being at the high school holding it in place and not getting any credit. Some staff members said that I left the high school out of spite to watch it fall apart in my stead. I just needed a change of not getting stepped on.

I knew that I would be running LV Moore because she didn't have a clue about what to do as a principal. She'd ask me about every little aspect of the job. I handled all discipline and supervised all three lunches/recesses. She showed her inability to lead in every aspect. The staff would bypass her and come to me. By March of that year, my new middle school boss was fired, the high school principal was fired, and the new superintendent of schools was fired. (She had replaced my so-called friend as superintendent after he retired).

A PRINCIPAL SHIP AND
NEW TRIALS AND TRIBULATIONS

My good friend and coworker Darlene Roberto, who was a sharp middle school principal, was appointed the new superintendent of schools. A day or so after all those people were fired, Darlene called me.

"Get your ass over to that high school and put it back in order."

Again a woman rescued me by making me a high school principal. Now I would have to run graduation for both schools.

When I walked into the high school, the teachers hugged me, and the students as a whole were glad to see me. That place was a mess. In the short time I was gone, the students didn't seem to care about the late bell. They hung out in the hallways, playing music, and a couple of gangs were wearing their colors on the sly.

On day one I was kicking ass and taking names, so to speak. I cleaned that mess up really quick, making examples out of those who thought that they could continue with their gangs and those who were chronically disruptive. I expelled some students, and with some I gave their parents an alternative: *Either take your son or daughter out of my school, or I will expel them*.

After things got quiet in the building, I held an assembly with the entire student body, and the first thing I said was, "Do you all notice that certain people are missing? If you don't want to come up missing, keep doing what you're doing."

The student body applauded along with the staff.

I said, "I'm your daddy while you are here. We are here to educate you. And as for me, I will treat you all equally as I always have, and I'll do anything for you in my power."

I kept my word all through the rest of my career.

Soon after I was hired as principal, Darlene and I reconfigured the administrative staff. Up until then the administrative staff consisted of the principal, two vice principals, and a chairperson for each academic discipline. We eliminated all department chairs with the exception of math and reading.

A Home Economics class baked me a birthday cake.

Darlene allowed me to hire four vice principals who had expertise in the departments where chairs were eliminated: English, math, science, liberal arts, history, etc. I hired seven vice principals during my six years as principal and not one had prior administrative experience because I believed hiring vice principals that wanted to make lateral moves sometimes spelled trouble. The one I hired all interviewed well with parents, teachers, and students involved in the process. I also believed in giving chances as I was given a chance.

I'm especially proud of Nathaniel Fisher who moved up the ladder to a higher position in the district. The one year I was a vice principal at L V Moore, Nathaniel teaching by day while also taking classes for his administrative credentials. He caught my attention because he reminded me of me. I witnessed him going far above and beyond his assigned duties; coupled with that, he had an admirable rapport with the student body and the teaching staff. I brought him to the high school in 1999 as vice principal. He eventually became principal, and today he is the superintendent of schools in that same district.

While principal I brought in the Junior Reserve Officers' Training Corps (JROTC), distance learning laboratory, computer labs, a mentoring program with AT&T professionals tutoring students after school, authored and implemented an alternative school, and an intergenerational day, which was a once-a-year program where the high school invited the town's senior citizens to be our guests for a sit-down luncheon. If the elderly didn't have transportation, we arranged to pick them up.

All the food would be cooked and served by our home economics classes. You name it, and it was on the menu. Our award-winning student nursing program would be on display, with the students taking vital signs at different stations or assisting those who needed help walking. Students mingled with the elderly and ate with them. Our Marine Corp JROTC drill team would also perform. Without my boss, Darlene Roberto, none of the aforementioned would have been possible. She went to bat for me on the funding beyond my school budget! She always had my back and knew that she could always count on me to have hers.

As principal I showed my appreciation to the staff by hosting catered picnics for the entire teaching staff, support staff, some central office workers, and friends—sometimes as many as 120 people. I also threw Christmas parties for staff members at times.

I guess I enjoy seeing people eating and enjoying themselves. Thinking about it, I've enjoyed giving in some way ever since adulthood, especially in the capacity as a teacher, department chairman, vice-principal, and principal. I'm no psychoanalyst, but I think I try to do the opposite of how I was treated growing up by my dad and relatives.

Even as principal I was still moonlighting and being a gentleman farmer. Now that I was getting to know my way around in the county, I hired another heavy equipment company to do some excavation for me. The company was family-owned, but the retired father, Elmer, came to my house to see what I wanted done. He admitted he came mainly out of curiosity. He told me he flew over my property every time he took off from the Somerset County Airport. He said he just had to see who owned this beautiful piece of property.

I remembered seeing him at the airport while I was taking flying lessons. We talked about flying so much that he almost forgot why he came to my house. Elmer was in his late seventies who didn't mind flaunting that he was a wealthy man, but rumor had it that he was the cheapest man alive. He invited me to fly with him, and of course I accepted. He owned a Piper Cherokee PA 28 four-passenger aircraft that costs a half-million dollars or more. Beautiful. We ended up being friends, and we flew many times together.

I had another friend, Gary, that I would hire to do some trenching and digging in wet places since he had a track hoe. I had no idea that he knew Elmer. One day while he was working for me, I told him that I had to leave to go flying, and the conversation led to Elmer Simon.

He said, "He's almost blind, and he crashed my uncle's Lear jet."

After that news, I always made sure I did the landing.

One Thursday evening Elmer called and asked if I wanted to take a weekend flight to Virginia with his best friend's son and son-in-law. They'd leave on Friday and come back Monday morning. I said that I would love to but, I had a commitment at my school. I was being honored at halftime at a football game that Saturday.

Before takeoff on Monday morning, Elmer was advised by the tower that it was pretty soupy up there, and he should wait until it cleared up before taking off. Elmer was always headstrong and stubborn, always bragging about the Piper's state-of-the-art instrumentation and that he was one of the best pilots. Ignoring the tower's warning, he took off and crashed, killing himself, his friend's son, and son-in-law.

A Piper Cherokee that I flew and that my good friend Elmer flew before he died in the crash.

I felt bad because had I been there, maybe I could have talked him out of it. Nevertheless, I'm still here, yet one more time I escaped meeting my maker. And I haven't flown a plane since.

A few days after Elmer's funeral, racism reared its ugly head again at my property. Early one morning I was leaving my house to get a load of hay. As I approached my gate, I noticed quite a few neighbors in front of my gate and stone stanchions. I got out of my truck to ask what was going on. They said they were cleaning some graffiti off of my gate. I walked around the wall to see what they were talking about and found the word nigger spray-painted on my stone walls, the shrubs, and driveway entrance. They had buckets of gas and brushes trying to erase the paint out of the porous stone.

I immediately told them to stop and called the police. I guessed that the neighborhood didn't want the publicity, so they took it upon themselves to clean the big, bold writing that was really visible from the road.

The police arrived and asked me who I thought would do that. I had no idea. They then suggested that someone on my job might be mad with me. I asked if they knew where I worked and what I did. They didn't.

"Don't insult my intelligence. I work thirty miles away, and I'm a high school principal."

They finished taking the statement and left. I drove away to get my hay. When I returned most of the graphite was gone. I continued down my driveway toward the barn and noticed four White guys in the distance crossing one of my pastures.

They were yelling, "Nigger, go back to where you came from."

They were so far away that they figured that I couldn't catch them on foot. But I was so infuriated I jumped out of my truck, and the chase was on. They had a quarter-mile lead on me, but those punks were out of shape and would pause for breath every so often while I continued jogging. I chased them through the woods and all parts of the neighborhood.

People would call, "Stop chasing those boys, or we'll call the police." I said, "Please do call the police."

This went on for quite some time. I finally chased them to a dead-end where three police cars were waiting. The police asked me what was going on, and I explained what took place on my property and what they were calling me. The boys were cuffed and taken away. Not once was I asked if I wanted to press charges for them defacing property.

As it had happened, the day I was honored at the football game, I was driving to the stadium in a new Porsche and was stopped by a Bridgewater policeman for speeding—going five miles per hour over the speed limit. There wasn't any reason for me to dispute him because he was going to write the citation regardless. I just took the citation and continued on to the game.

A couple of weeks later, not long after I chased down the four racists, I went to pay the ticket and happened to run across the chief of police. I asked to speak with him, and he asked me what he could do for me. I said I was there for my five miles over the speed limit ticket, but I wanted to know whatever happened with the racial vandalism from two weeks earlier. I was still waiting to hear from someone.

He was totally lost for words and asked me what I did for a living. I said I was a high school principal. He said that in his job like mine, we couldn't talk about certain things that happen. Bullshit. I answered by saying the infraction happened to me. He still wouldn't give me a straight answer. I mentioned how I hadn't gone to the media back then and was trying very hard not to do so now. That got his attention. He promised to get back to me as soon as he could. He also asked to see the speeding ticket and tore it up.

The following day I was in my office at the high school when my secretary told me that the mayor of Bridgewater was on the phone. The chief of police had probably told him that I was going to cause problems over the racist defacing of my property that they apparently thought was moot.

When I said hello, he introduced himself and asked where I worked. He seemed surprised to learn I was a principal. At the planning board meetings, he had always treated me like I was dirt or some homeless bum. Or maybe he was just outright prejudiced.

I always gave the benefit of the doubt to most people, and most of the time I got knocked down for it. After I told him what I did for a living, I threw a couple of big names at him that I rubbed elbows with. I also told him that I was friends with the county chief of police.

He then warmed up to me, and by the way he carried on, you'd have thought we were the best of friends. He then went on to tell me that the case was still pending, but he would keep me abreast and apologized for the delay. I knew it was all a bunch of crap and was going nowhere. I didn't call the newspapers or push the issue; instead, I figured I'd use this as leverage down the road.

And life went on.

As I mentioned before, it seemed that the code enforcement department of the township was knocking on my door every time I started a bulldozer or backhoe since sound travels. Sometimes the inspector would show up after one of my friends who owned a dump truck had come for a visit. The complaint was that there was illegal dumping on my property, which wasn't true. Every time I would ask who made the complaint, they would say that they couldn't say.

There were several occasions when animal control would come calling because of complaints that my two Labradors were loose in the neighborhood, which wasn't true most of the time as they could see the dogs in their large run. The constant false accusations finally took a toll on both officers, and one of them finally told me.

"It's the Franklins making the complaints."

The Franklins lived just off Meadow Road, 1,100 feet away from my house. It would be impossible for Superman to see through the thickly wooded boundary. There was a small stream that ran along the right side of my driveway, which would be part of their backyard as far as they were concerned. But according to my survey, it was my property. They dammed up the stream, creating a small pond with a spillway that babbled as a relaxation sound. I guess they didn't know they were breaking the law by blocking the stream and that they were on my property. I never said a word because I'm a turn the other cheek kind of guy.

Did I mention that they had a huge pile of dirt from digging the pond that was still there and was eroding into the stream? Talk about breaking code. I said nothing, but I did have one of my senior students come to the house for a job one Saturday to help around the farm. He drove my old dump truck while I operated my backhoe. I removed that pile of dirt as a good neighbor would. I could see them peeking out of the window but never came out. Is it possible there was a little guilt involved? The following Monday evening when I arrived home from work, I found four large pots of chrysanthemums on my front porch without a note. No need to guess where they came from. I did thank them one day while passing them as they sat at their retreat.

A coworker of a former student found it hard to believe that the Franklins would be so vindictive because they were very religious Catholics. (They attended the same church.) Mrs. Franklin was a communion steward. Were they hypocrites or prejudiced?

Mr. Vanilli, who owned the company that installed my in-ground pool, was also a neighbor, and we became friends. Every time that he would see me, he would ask me to come to his church. I finally took him up on it. He met me outside then we went in and joined his wife. It was a beautiful, huge church. Even though it was ultra-modern, it appeared and felt as if God himself were present.

After the homily I noticed that Mrs. Franklin was there, giving the

Eucharist. It just so happened that I was in her line, and I loved that she would have to give me Eucharist. The look on her face when I stepped up to her ...

I attended that church until I moved to West Virginia. I guess that there is a reason for everything, even if I haven't figured it out as of yet.

As principal, I would often confer with Katie Coles, director of special services, and we became friends over the years. She was best of friends with Linda Vestal, Somerset County's first female chief of police who was Black, so she made double history. I invited Linda to be a guest speaker for a woman in power all-girl assembly at my school. After that we became friends, and she had been to my farm on a couple of occasions.

Linda was good friends with Christine Todd Whitman, who would be running for governor of New Jersey in 1994. Linda thought that my place would be a nice backdrop for a fundraiser for Whitman, with my kidney-shaped pool, covered patio, expansive manicured yard, and views of pastures with horses and cows grazing, the pond, and a mini-park on a hillside adjacent to the back yard adorned with plants, benches, and a gazebo at the top of the hill.

I agreed, and Governor Whitman held a beautiful invitation-only affair at my residence. If you donated, you received a ticket for drinks and hors d'oeuvres. I also had a live jazz band, who were four of my former students. Everyone there was dressed in business attire and evening dresses. Governor Whitman gave a short speech, and we were formally introduced. She never forgot who I was. After she became governor, I was invited to her annual Toys for Tots Christmas parties every year. Mentioning her name as a friend would help me in the future.

After being in my principalship for a few years, negotiation time came around, and I asked for a $5,000 raise instead of the $3,000 raise that the Board of Education wanted to give me. I was fifty-five and had just about worked enough years to retire—the formula then was to be fifty-five with thirty years of service. I had twenty-nine plus years. Had the board given me what I wanted, I might have stuck around for a couple of years longer. Since I'd done well between moonlighting, the subdivisions, the stock market, and my principal's salary, I decided to retire.

The woman who replaced me was a PhD and impressed the board with all of her Neverland ideas. There was some nepotism mixed in there also. She shadowed me for the last two months of the school year, and she had an air about her that was rather haughty and snobbish, making it clear she thought she didn't need my advice.

Me feeding some of my cattle

I retired in June 2002 and became a full-time gentleman farmer. I had several staff members call me to complain about their new boss, wishing that I were back there. All I could do was laugh and tell them that they had no idea how good it felt without all that pressure.

In January 2003 Darlene Roberto called and asked me to come back and finish out the school year as principal because the PhD had been fired, and the high school was a complete mess. I really didn't want to come back, but I did it for Darlene because without her I would have never become principal in the first place. Besides, it would only be for six months, and the per diem would be good.

Darlene didn't tell the high school staff that I was coming back, so they didn't know who to expect after the Christmas vacation. When I walked into the building, the students and teachers were again hugging me. I brought things back to order, had a smooth school closing, and made my exit.

That summer I received a call from the Board of Education president asking me if I would consider coming out of retirement. He said that they would give me the salary I wanted. I turned down the offer went about my retirement. And now was the time to cash in on the police department's lack of action on the vandalism at my property years before. Knowing I had them over a barrel, I called the mayor and said I wanted to purchase a parcel next door to me that was landlocked, and my driveway would be the access to three lots. I then asked him what he thought, and he said it was a good idea. I asked him if he was going to get in my way again, and he assured me I wouldn't have any problems. That's all I wanted to hear, and we said goodbye.

BETRAYAL BY ANOTHER FRIEND

A few weeks before I had the conversation with the mayor, I had inquired about the five-acre parcel for sale by my neighbors, the Zegars, that ran parallel to the left of my driveway. The land was landlocked. I figured that I would buy the land and use my driveway as a common road to branch off of. If I could purchase this parcel, it would give me access to a lot that I already owned on the other side.

I remember encountering some elderly Black men fishing on my property when I first purchased it. They asked me who I was. I told them I was the new owner but didn't mind them fishing. You'd have thought I had just given them the deed to the property. They were so happy a Black man owned a big piece of property in the area. They didn't hesitate to tell me about the many times they'd been called nigger any time they drove down my road.

When I saw the for-sale sign in the Zegar's yard, I went and knocked on their door. Mr. Zegar answered. I told him that I was interested in his five acres and would pay the asking price of $85,000. He immediately said that the property wasn't for sale any longer and more or less shut the door in my face. I guess I was supposed to say okey-doke because we ignorant Blacks wouldn't know any different.

I smelled a rat, so I went to my engineer friend Bob, explained the situation, and he volunteered to buy the property in my stead if it was indeed still for sale. I actually had some other White friends who had told me they would buy the parcel for me, but I accepted Bob's offer since he'd be doing the engineering work anyway and going to the planning board with me.

Bob went to see Zegar, who was more than glad to sell the property to him. Bob even haggled him down to $80,000. Jackpot. They later signed a contract pending the regular red tape. When it went through, I'd be able to put two lots along the driveway and the third that I already owned on the side of the property. This would mean at least $325,000 per lot ($975,000) plus a piece of the houses since I would help build them. Building lots were in high demand in Bridgewater at that time.

Before the closing, Bob did all of the surveying and the subdivisions on paper to have them ready the day the deal closed. I didn't bother Bob for more than a month and a half, thinking he would call me for a check to close the deal. I finally got restless and went to his office to see what the status was. He told me that he'd let the contract run out and got a two-week extension.

They were waiting for him to purchase the property. What was he thinking? But being one who takes a man at his word, I stayed fairly calm and figured the deal would close any day. After a few days I went to Bob's office again. He told me that he let the deal go because of ethics—because he was fronting for me. I hit the ceiling, thinking that first my so-called friend in education did me in, and now Bob turned out to be another so-called friend.

I thought that I was going to have a heart attack. I couldn't talk I was so upset, especially since those two White women would have purchased the property for me. When I told my two female friends what had happened, they both cried and apologized as if it were their fault. What hurts the most is that I already had the mayor set up to grant this new subdivision.

Shortly after I lost the deal, I received a phone call from a local contractor. I didn't know him, but I knew of him. He told me that he had purchased the five-acre parcel next door to me, and he needed an easement from me. It literally knocked the wind out of me, thinking that my engineer and this man had done a number on me. After I gathered my thoughts, I asked what he could do for me. He asked me what I wanted, and I said a twenty-foot wide and thirty-foot long easement in order for me to get to a building lot that his property blocked me from getting to. He agreed immediately as if he already knew that's what I'd want.

If I were to pursue this venture, I would definitely have to find another engineer. The one thing I wouldn't do was give up part of my driveway for his access. If I granted that, my private electronic gate would have to be torn down. I'm guessing they figured out my driveway wasn't on the table. A couple of months later, I discovered that the township agreed that he could use Mr. Zegar's existing narrow driveway as access to his lot, which was unheard of.

My friend Martin Limbeck from Germany wrote the bestseller *Why Nobody Wants You to Get to the Top*. In the book he states that sometimes your best friend may be the enemy within. He was so right. I experienced that with my education career and again with my engineer.

That big letdown simmered inside of me for a few months. I finally decided it was time to move on.

GETTING OUT OF DODGE

I listed the house with a realty company knowing it could take forever to sell, especially to someone White. I already milked the property for just about all I could get out of it, with the exception of the four acres the house sat on and the twenty-nine acres of manicured pastures, woodland, and a four-horse barn on the flood plain.

But three days after publishing the listing, I had four inquiries. Two of the inquiries were just curious. One inquiry was serious but no deal. The fourth inquiry loved everything—the privacy, manicured pastures, the house with all the amenities—and said he'd take it. There was no haggling, and I got the price that I wanted. I explained I was keeping a two-acre plot that was about two hundred yards away, straight across the front lawn. That new house would be facing his house. He said he would not buy my house unless he had total privacy. He did not want to see another house facing him. He wanted the property as it looked at present. He then asked how much I wanted for those two acres. I told him $375,000, but the lot had not been approved by the planning board yet.

He didn't care. He bought that lot too. So altogether I walked away with well over $2 million. We agreed I'd get six months to move out, and he'd put $500,000 in escrow. The realtor drew up the agreement, and we both signed it.

Those six months went by fast. I soon found myself with a time problem. I had horses, cattle, and farm equipment to sell or give away and four cars to move. That six-month period went by really fast. I did sell some of the farm equipment, gave away some, sold one horse, gave away two, and kept the horse, which my friend in Harding Township would take care of.

Over those six months I traveled several times to Weirton, West Virginia, where my college buddy and best friend Larry lived, and looked at many used and new houses, but none were to my liking. I did find an upscale development called Angelina Estates that I liked. The part I was interested in was an extension of the development that had some million-dollar-plus houses on it. The Weirton Medical Center was walking distance away, and most of those upscale houses belonged to doctors, mainly from Pennsylvania. Pittsburgh was only thirty minutes away, and some of the doctors were residents in both Pittsburgh hospitals and in Weirton Medical. Some built their houses in West Virginia because of cheaper property taxes, which in the Pittsburgh metropolitan area were insane.

Most of the new houses there were beautiful but with limited privacy. I found two adjacent lots on the end of the development that would give me privacy with no houses in the rear. I was going to buy the two lots until I looked through the trees and saw a Serbian Center with a parking lot. No deal. I was spoiled after having near fifty acres of total privacy.

My friend Larry had lived in Weirton all of his life. He started out as a guidance counselor then moved up to an assistant principal in a junior high, the principal of the same school, and finally an assistant superintendent directing maintenance and grounds. He knew just about everyone in the town. He introduced me to two of his former students—one a lawyer and the other a doctor. Their deceased father had built a real estate empire in Weirton. They owned several hundred units of apartments, office buildings, a motel in Florida, hundreds of acres of land in Weirton among other properties.

Their father also built each of the three siblings a new brick home as gifts. I hit it off right away with the doctor and was invited to his house a couple of times. After I told him that I was searching for property, he agreed to show me a seventy-five-acre parcel. His mother had agreed to let him sell it so he could invest in a real estate deal in Florida.

The parcel was the remains of a small development located at the base of a hill. The property would start with about twenty approved lots with gas, water, and electric. A quarter of a mile up a beautiful, paved road, almost at the top of the hill, was a million-dollar-plus house with an electric estate gate and the yard fronted with a wrought iron fence. The paved road ended there in a cul-de-sac.

Off to the right was a grassy incline about a hundred yards or so to the summit. Perfect. I could see my modern house with plenty of glass sitting up there looking down on the house below—Black king of the hill. The house on the cul-de-sac used to belong to the lawyer brother who sold it to a casino tycoon who spent an additional $1 million in improvements and often entertained the high rollers of the casino.

I wanted this property with a passion, no matter what the cost. I could see myself building some moderate-priced houses at the base of the hill to match the existing houses to recoup some of the money paid for the parcel.

He asked for $450,000. I agreed without hesitation, and we shook on it. I told him to draw up the papers, and I'd return with a certified check in five days. He also told me about a two-hundred-acre parcel that he called wasteland because there were no utilities anywhere near the property. He said that he would take $1,000 per acre. I was so psyched about the dream parcel that I didn't even look at it. I drove back to New Jersey to get the money. The day after I returned home, I got a phone call from the doctor. He was the bearer of bad news. He stated that his big brother the lawyer was their mother's favorite, and he squashed the deal by talking the mother out of it. What a downer for me.

I'm now in deep thought, wondering what in the hell was wrong with me. Was it my skin color again? Was it because the doctor was pulling my leg about the sale of the property, thinking the price was out of my league? Was it that the family didn't want to sell to a Black man? I still believed that this was the land of opportunity for all people because I continued to give the benefit of the doubt.

But giving benefit of the doubt left me with the mental anguish of wondering while life goes on for the person causing the pain of the doubt. I found out later that the family didn't want to sell to me for whatever reason, but they sold it to someone else for less money, and that person wasn't Black. You are smart enough to draw your own conclusions. I was left with the pain of asking God: *Why me?* I was told that the two hundred acres he supposedly wanted to sell me were sold. The new owner got rich from oil and gas leases. Good for the new owners, good for the sellers in a bad way, and tough luck for me.

STUPID MOVE AND GOOD MOVE

I finally closed on my New Jersey home, placed my furniture in temperature-controlled storage, and temporarily moved in with Larry in Weirton. At that time in 2003, there was a mad rush on legal gambling. I was interested because the slot machines seemed like a quick buck. Larry and I decided to look for a decent building in downtown Weirton.

We found a brick building with a sound structure for $85,000. Quite a few of Larry's former White students told us they had gotten business loans to get their "cafés" started—the state didn't allow these places to be called gambling houses or mini-casinos. The state allowed you to have five machines per building. We went to one of the local banks and couldn't go wrong because Larry knew everyone there.

I could have easily paid cash for the building, but we would need a write-off. We asked for a $120,000 loan. After we went through the whole application process, we were asked what we had for collateral. We thought the building itself would be enough, but they said no. I whipped out two seven-figure bank accounts, but they wouldn't accept that. My money wasn't good enough because apparently, I might blow it away. They made Larry put his house up, which was valued at $160,000. And they also wanted him to put up his rental property, appraised at $40,000. So Larry had to put up two houses for $200,000 collateral for an $85,000 building. They assured us that after we made improvements on the building and if it came in higher than $85,000, they would remove the liens from his homes.

The closing was handled by the bank rep's son, who seemed shady.

We discovered that it wasn't a business loan but a personal loan. It didn't matter because we probably had a lawsuit. We played stupid and rolled with the punches. If a push came to a shove, I would pay the building off.

I was wrong thinking that I could bring a touch of New York to that shoddy little steel town. I put up an extra $120,000 of my money and would do much of the work myself and subcontract the remainder. It took a few months to get a liquor and gambling license.

Our attorney was one of Larry's former students, whose family owned about ten of these cafes. They were a well-to-do family, and he did all of our initial paperwork pro bono. The building had an attached two-car garage but without an entrance into the main building. The club shared a common wall with the garage that would make a perfect casino separate from the club. They say that the little old ladies who were the best gambling customers didn't like to walk into bars to play slot machines. My vision was to cut an entrance through the concrete wall, remove the garage doors and replace with a wall and front door. The problem was that the budget wouldn't allow it.

One day while I was working in the club, a young gentleman entered and asked if the owner was around. I raised my hand, and we talked. He wanted to be the vendor for all of our games, pool tables, slot machines, entertainment electronics, and ATM machines. His name was Dave, and it just so happened that his grandfather had supplied my dad's club years ago.

Dave asked what I needed. I told him my idea about the garage project. He said that he would give me $20,000 toward the project. What a blessing. We remodeled that new room with big smoked glass front windows, Vegas carpet, smoke eaters, air conditioning, and a touch of Vegas depicted on the walls. Beautiful.

We named the club Crossroads because it was located on the corner. It was totally new inside with nice touches outside. It had two large bathrooms with one handicap equipped, a full-service kitchen, carpeted dining area, oak dance floor, televisions, high-powered speakers on the walls of the dance floor and in the ceiling, and pool tables upstairs in a room that would be used for private parties. The club had lights covering the entire outside front of the club along the

roofline. We also had mock electric traffic lights on the walls inside. The inside walls were black and white, adorned with multiple framed pictures of New York. People would ask what professionals decorated the place.

Crossroads was the talk of the town. We made nice profits the first two years between the kitchen, bar, gambling, and games. I got $25,000 of my investment back. We had a respectable clientele that included nurses, doctors, and casino workers from the Mountaineer Casino. We were pen for lunch and dinner. There was Friday night dancing with a DJ and a jazz trio on Wednesdays with no cover charge. We had two waiters and a bartender on two shifts who were probably robbing us blind.

Larry and I were never there during the day because I was busy building my house, and Larry hadn't retired from his day job yet. All we did was drop in once in a while. I also purchased a condominium in Costa Rica that was still under construction and would take frequent trips there to check out the progress. Neither of us had any business trying to run a club. You have to almost live there to make a profit. We were just donating to the community by keeping some people employed and spreading goodwill.

One Wednesday evening on jazz night, a small-statured man came into the club with his personal bodyguard/chauffeur to listen to the music. He bought a round of drinks for everyone in the house and introduced himself as Ted Arneau, CEO of the Mountaineer Casino and

Resort. He was also the guy who lived on the cul-de-sac of the hill that I had wanted to purchase.

Ted turned out to be a really nice guy and would show up just about every Wednesday and set up the house. We became friends, and his influence brought the casino attorney—a former student of Larry's—and a troop of girls every Friday night to take in the dance floor, spending money like water. We also had a group of nurses who frequented our establishment and started holding their annual Christmas parties upstairs. The joint was jumping.

Another lawyer who was also one of Larry's former students, had sold his home to Ted. During that time he allegedly joked: Take my wife too. And apparently Ted did just that. She was a real looker that the attorney had met in Pittsburgh. As far as I know, she still lives in that same house on the hill.

Since Ted frequented our club, I just had to ask him if he'd had anything to do with me being turned down for the purchase of the property where he resides.

"Hell, no. I swear on my mother, it wasn't me. I would never do anything like that. If you could afford to buy that property and live there, more power to you. You could be my neighbor anytime."

After that, we were invited to his home on the hill for annual Christmas parties. They were black-tie or suit and tie affairs. There was valet parking and all the trimmings: coat check, wandering cocktails, hors d'oeuvres—the whole nine yards.

Everybody who was anybody was there: businessmen, lawyers, doctors, and politicians. I was hanging with the big dogs. He personally plucked me out of the crowd to let people know that I was his newfound friend. He always would tease me by saying that he was going to kick my ass, knowing that would be impossible. I looked like a giant standing beside him.

He kind of ignored his house full of guests and took me into his private study to show off his skills on the bass fiddle and the piano since he was a jazz buff. Boy that was a grueling twenty minutes. He wasn't proficient at all on either instrument. As we would walk through the crowded house, the looks on the guest's faces appeared to say: *Who in the hell is this Black guy that he's giving so much attention to?* Of course, some of them would make it their business to find out.

I was also invited to a steak dinner at the casino for Joe Manchin, who was running for governor at that time. Again, everybody who was anybody was there. They were all Democrats, and little did they know I was a Republican. The free dinner was very good.

One day I was flying back from Costa Rica to Pittsburgh. I was in an aisle seat, and two young ladies sat to my right talked the whole trip. One young lady was discussing her disdain for her dad's new girlfriend.

"He left my mother for that bimbo."

The other girl said, "How could Ted do that to his family."

Hearing the name Ted aroused my curiosity.

I dared to ask the young lady, "Excuse me, but I couldn't help but hear you talking about a man named Ted. By any chance are you talking about Ted Arneau?"

Her eyes went wide. "Oh, my God. Do you know him?"

"Yes, he's a friend of mine."

A while later I read in the paper that Ted Arneau had gotten divorced and had to pay his estranged wife a $30 million settlement as part of the divorce. Love is blind.

After a few years we started attracting a different clientele, and business at the club started falling off sharply. We had to start cutting back by getting rid of an accountant who was ripping us off, firing some bartenders and barmaids that were ripping us off. We were going to the State store every other day to restock. The manager of that liquor store crunched the numbers for me, and I am ashamed to say how much we were losing. One of our best White barmaids blew the whistle on another White barmaid who was ripping us off big time, giving free drinks to her boyfriend, his friends, and all of his relatives. We did away with live jazz and no more complimentary snacks on the bar and tables. Our girls from the casino stopped coming, as did the nurses and doctors.

I was in the mall one day and ran across the attorney for the casino and a friend of hers. I asked where they'd been. After some coaxing they reluctantly told me why they didn't come around anymore.

"There were a few Black girls who threatened to kick our asses if we keep coming to your club."

I was floored hearing this information. But Larry also heard it from another group of people. We found out that some of the people we thought were our friends were chasing people away. We lost one of our best barmaids to a bar down the street.

The owners of that bar, who were supposed to be Larry's friends, asked her, "Why do you work for these niggers? Come and work for us where there are more White people, and you will make much more money."

She did go there, but a month later she asked for her job back. She confessed she left because she was offered much more money and not because of the racial remarks. But she said she was still waiting to be paid for the first time. Not one of our employees ever had to wait for their paycheck.

During the period of owning that bar, I owned a new H2 Hummer, a Jaguar convertible, and a used Rolls Royce that I purchased from a lawyer friend in New Jersey. I was told that I shouldn't drive those vehicles to the club because people would get envious and stop coming to the club. Some of our Black clientele stopped coming and went to a bar down the street with a large rebel flag displayed in the entrance. Go figure. Some of the Black patrons told me that my secret name was Richie Rich.

Our club went straight to hell over the few years of ownership. In order to keep afloat, we resorted to hip-hop and rap music on Friday nights only. The young locals said that all those guys coming in the club from Steubenville, Ohio, were drug dealers from Chicago that spent money like water. They were very respectful to the barmaid, giving big tips.

The locals had little money and were jealous of those guys. Not once did those guys fight or start a fight. It would be the locals that would start trouble. The Steubenville guys assured us that they wouldn't start anything because they didn't want to mess up their Friday night good thing.

Most of the locals had very little money to spend and stood around as spectators. I hated every minute of this nonsense, but it was paying the bills. We had a few arguments, a couple of female fights, but the police only had to be called four times over the years. Business was getting so bad that I had to borrow $15,000 online to keep afloat. We were taking the cut of all the entertainment devices to help make ends meet, but the employees still got paid on time.

More than ever neither Larry nor I wanted to be there. We'd find the sinks torn off the bathroom walls, toilets stopped up, urine on the carpet upstairs leaking through the bar and restaurant ceiling. It was total sabotage. I was looking for any excuse to get the hell out of that mess.

One Friday the club was packed. There was a scuffle outside between two guys from Steubenville who were too young to enter the club and two adult locals who were troublemakers most of the time. The young boys were kicking their asses. Now that most of the people in the club were from Steubenville, they were trying to go outside to either help or act as spectators. I announced that if anyone went outside, they'd stay outside. So the people who were inside ran to the windows to watch but didn't try to force their way out past Larry and me standing in the doorway.

The two local adults that were supposed to be badasses were crawling on their hands and knees trying to get into the club. I would not let them in and had the barmaid call the police. To this day I don't know why Larry went out the door, which caused a flash flood of people to rush the door, which I couldn't hold shut by myself.

The two adults crawled in while my partner got punched in the jaw outside by who knows who. The crowd went into a frenzy. I was trying to quell all the fights going on inside with bottles flying, chairs flying, drinks flying, tables tossed, screaming, and yelling. We finally cleared the building, and then the police finally showed up.

That was it. I announced Crossroads was closed forever. I paid the employees and locked the doors for good.

I was stuck with the $15,000 loan that was in my name and was out $100,000 of my personal money. But I didn't care; closing those doors was a total relief. The hard part was telling Dave, the owner of all of the vending machines in the club. I was sure he hadn't recouped the $20,000 he gave me for the garage conversion to a casino.

The kitchen equipment, expensive vents on the roof, furniture, computerized cash register, bar equipment, and glasses had to be worth at least $60,000. I had a couple of companies give bids that weren't anywhere close to what the equipment was worth. I then called my friend Dave; his company also bought used bar and restaurant equipment. Dave came to the club and asked what I wanted for everything in there. I told him that all I wanted from him was a check for $13,300.

He said, "You're kidding."

"Is that too much?"

"Hell, no. I can't take all of this for that small amount."

I said, "Dave, I appreciate what you've done for me with your generous gift and all the times you came and set up the bar for all that were in here."

He cut me a check, and I never went back in the place again.

I'm one who doesn't blame anyone but myself for my stupid mistakes. I should have known better after witnessing what my dad went through years ago. The difference between my dad and I was he stayed in his club every hour that the club was open. Even though he was an abuser, he allowed no swearing and no disrespecting women—do as I say, not what I do. If you violated his wishes, you were barred for good. That would eliminate quite a few. The envious and the haters were either barred or went somewhere else. The kicker is if they went somewhere else, they acted like perfect ladies and gentlemen, just like our customers did when they stopped coming to my club to go to the rebel flag bar.

Thinning out the haters and envious caused the good clientele—Black and White—to stay in my dad's place, and everyone was happy, just like on the TV series *Cheers*.

When I was a principal, I once asked my math chairman why some of my math scores weren't up to par. He said you can't make chicken salad out of chicken shit. That applied to our club as well.

REBUILDING IN WEIRTON

After the farce over that seventy-five-acre hill I had wanted so badly, I heard about Sam Cusic, an attorney who owned large parcels of land Weirton. He was a former state senator who owned a chain of restaurants, buildings that he leased, and hundreds of acres of virgin, mostly hilly, land.

Several people told me *Good luck* in trying to buy anything from Sam because he was a hoarder and wouldn't sell anything to anybody. I didn't quite know how to take that. I wasn't sure if they were trying to tell me as nicely as they knew how that he wouldn't sell to me because I was Black. If I called him, he might say: *Yes, I have land available*, but then maybe after he saw me, he would come up with some demeaning excuse. I've been there before, and it's a damn shame that anyone in the land of the free has to even have to ponder like this. I decided to show my Black face in person. That way it would be either yes or no, and he could carry on as usual, and my feelings wouldn't be hurt.

Contrary to what I was told, he said that he'd be happy to show me a few places. He was a very nice guy, as far as I could glean. He loved the outdoors, wildlife, and trees, as evidenced by observing the back of his new Jaguar SUV that he didn't mind neglecting with tree branches, acorns, pinecones, and samples of different tree logs. We connected quickly because I had two Jaguars, and he had four—one each for his wife, himself, and two daughters. I explained that I was looking for privacy, and he took me to a twenty-two-acre mountain with no access.

In order to get to the base of this mountain, you had to drive through a neatly kept development that he and his father had built twenty or thirty years before. They were now selling it for $152,000 to $200,000-plus. A final wing of this development would take you up a moderate steep road about a quarter of a mile in length. There was no way that any vehicle could possibly negotiate that wooded hill.

Sam took off his street shoes, changed into his hiking boots, and up the hill we hiked. He said that he always wanted to build his home on top of the hill but wouldn't know how to get up there. When we reached the top, you could see for miles in all directions. I was imagining myself being like the Grinch with Whoville below me. I wondered if he was showing me the mountain because he thought I wouldn't want it because there was no access or if he was for real. The top of that hill was razor back in shape, and it would take some tree clearing and leveling dirt to have space for a large house, yard, and possibly a barn.

Three sides of the mountain were steep terrain, and the fourth side was a cliff dropping straight down with a road and creek below. You could hear the echo of the creek babbling since there were no leaves on the trees. I already imagined the setup of my future home. The rear of the house would have a steel beam framed deck extending over that cliff to give a sensation of hanging out in space. I liked the property already.

He went as far as to say that if I cut a rough road to the top, he would pay for it if I bought the property or not. He had no idea who he was talking to. When it came to dirt, I could do anything after what my dad had put me through growing up using only picks and shovels. Give me machinery, and I'll move mountains. I wondered about his motive. Was he just looking for a place to camp and hike after I get the dirty work completed? Regardless, I would take the challenge, even if I had to rent a dozer myself.

As luck would have it, my buddy Larry was overseeing a project at a high school football stadium. A contracting company out of Pennsylvania was adding bleachers and doing some landscaping at that stadium. Surely, they had to have some heavy equipment. I was only a couple miles from where Larry was, so I drove over there. When I arrived at the stadium, there happened to be a new D-8 bulldozer sitting there doing nothing.

I told Larry what I had in mind, and we went over and explained it to the owner of the construction company. The contractor asked me if I had time to go look at the mountain at this moment. Of course I said yes. We drove to the mountain in his pickup truck. He studied the hill for a minute, and we walked a potential road—and used the same route that I had in mind. He told me that he would put a man on it the next day if it was alright with me—words I liked to hear.

I asked him what the financial damage would be, and he said he wouldn't kill me because he was already in the area with the machinery. He said it shouldn't take his best man more than a half a day to cut the rough road, and if it took longer, he would still charge only for a half-day because I was a friend of Larry's.

He jokingly said, "When my man is finished with this road, you should be able to drive your Porsche up this road."

The following morning I showed up, and the equipment showed up. The driver was an elderly man who told me that he'd been with the company for forty years. I left it up to him to negotiate that hill. I sat and watched the old man for hours until he reached the summit. That same day I brought my 4x4 pickup truck to be the first to drive that new road. It didn't appear to be that steep because I was excited. It's like buying a new pair of shoes that you really like, and they don't hurt when you try them on in the store, but when you get them home and put them on, they hurt your feet.

After he finished the rough road, the boss showed up, and we squared up in cash. He then told me that if I needed him in the near future, he'd still be in the area for a week or so and would make the road like a regular driveway because his gigantic roller compactor was in town with him. All I had to do was order the heavy underlayment (heavy six-inch slag/gravel) and the crush and run (¾-inch gravel mixed with stone dust) for the topping.

I drove to Cusic's office and asked if he had time to take a ride with me to the property because I needed to know some boundaries to have the temporary road cut. He said okay but took his own vehicle so he could go straight home from there. That was actually perfect because he had no idea that the road was already cut, and when we arrived he could drive his own vehicle up that road. He followed me to the property and followed me up that driveway, and when we reached the top and got out of our vehicles, he was more excited than I was. I told him that I was serious about buying the parcel and asked him how much he had in mind for twenty acres of the mountain. He said that he would get back to me that evening.

You'd have to be a mountain goat to build anywhere on the sides of that mountain. I was just interested in leveling off the top enough to accomplish what I had in mind and maybe enough room on the top for my son to build a house if he chose to do so. He called me that evening with a price and asked if I thought it was too much. That was a first. I had expected to pay more and took the deal. He then said that he would discount the difference for the rough road. He told me that he would have a contract drawn up in the morning since he was the realtor, the title company, and the lawyer. I signed the contract that following day. Even though the deal would take a couple of weeks to close, he said I could start clearing and get a head start on the driveway so the lumber and concrete trucks could get up there.

We shook on the deal, and I was on it that same day. I went to see the contractor to put the finishing touches on the road. He said he'd order the stone and just charge me the contractor's wholesale price. Now he was talking my language.

I already had my building plans approved and gave a copy to the company that helped me remodel the club. I liked their work, and they pointed me in the direction of plumbers, electricians, masons, excavators, sheet rockers, painters, lumber yard, etc. Within a month, I had the construction moving like clockwork. I was also a subcontractor and a worker. The road was completed and smooth as glass because the contractor let me use the compactor for an additional weekend, so I drove it up and down that driveway the entire weekend. There were a couple of hard rains to test the driveway, but there were no washouts whatsoever.

I decided to spend a little more money and ordered custom-made foundation walls from a company called Superior Walls that used concrete with wooden studs pressed into the interior of the walls for sheetrock. There were also predrilled holes for electric and plumbing. The company came, took a set of plans, and had every detail made at the plant. My job was to dig the footings and fill them with clean ¾ inch gravel two feet thick. No concrete was necessary for the footings. The walls arrived a couple of weeks later on tractor-trailers. A huge crane lowered the walls on the gravel footings while the ground crew bolted the walls together. It was finished in a few hours.

We were framing that same day. A local lumber yard that my carpenters always used spoon-fed us the lumber like clockwork. I wanted the house finished by December, and it was already June. I was like the conductor of a well-equipped orchestra. The framing, the sheathing, the roofing, the electric, the plumbing—all the workers were on it.

I'd built houses quite a few times over the previous twenty years, but you need to know what you're doing, otherwise don't. People try subcontracting their own house, thinking they'll save tons of money. But without experience you can end up paying much more and taking much more time to complete the job.

By December 2005 I was on my self-projected schedule because I worked day and night clearing up loose ends. Once I had heat, electric, water, gas, and bathrooms, I could move in and finish up within. I'd finish the amenities outside in the spring.

When I got into my house, the racism started. I'd come home and find the word *nigger* sprayed on some of my trees, probably by some young aspiring racists because whoever did it had to walk up the mountain to deface my trees—my electronic estate gate was four hundred fifty feet from the top of the hill. I also would find hunting arrows broken and lying beside the house, some stuck in the yard, and a couple stuck in the garage roof. The arrows that were broken had probably hit the brick walls.

An elderly White lady who lived in the neighborhood below told an acquaintance that I was running a house of ill repute because a White girl was going up there. She also said that that the cops were my best customers because they could go through his gate anytime they want. (Both the police and fire department had access codes to my gate for obvious reasons.) There were also rumors that I was selling drugs because of my house and cars.

I heard through a very reliable source that the Weirton police did run a check on me because I was the only Black man in town with fancy cars that would be parked at the club. The policemen that came to my house on their own were county policemen since I didn't live in Weirton's city limits. The policemen would come most of the time in the winter. Ice would build up under some windows and expand, causing the window to lose contact with the sensors, resulting in a very loud exterior alarm sounding. This would mostly happen while I was away in Costa Rica.

In order to get to my house, you either had access to my gate or climb up the mountain through the woods. So none of the neighbors had seen my house. A group of them must have thought I wasn't home and decided to trespass and climb the mountain together. I came home to find twelve adults standing there like deer in the headlights. I got out of my car and asked if I could help them. They said that they were just looking at my house. Another man might have gotten mad and raised hell, but it was par for the course for me. After that encounter I heard remarks like:

Why would he build a house like that in a neighborhood with menial homes like ours; he'll never get his money back if he sells, etc.

They all looked past the total privacy that some people would be looking for in a home. It would also be a hunter's paradise. I was banking on just that, should I decide to sell. This luxury home came with seventy-five hundred square feet of living space, six fireplaces, gourmet kitchen with commercial refrigerator with three ovens, two mini kitchens both with wet bars, library, mother-in-law suite, indoor ten-foot waterfall and pond, indoor pool, three furnaces and air conditioners, five bedrooms, two master closets, vaulted ceilings with many skylights, five and a half baths, a weight room, a two-hundred bottle wine refrigerator in the pool spa room, a home theatre, a fifteen hundred bottle wine cellar, a large deck protruding over a cliff, an outdoor putting green with three sand traps, fire pit with patio, in-ground pool, barn, outdoor kitchen, and estate gate with cameras and PA system.

I finished the house and all the outdoor landscaping and amenities by 2007. I spent most of my time alone. I'd see Larry and his son to ride our Harleys and golf. Other than that I'd be at my condo in Costa Rica. The only other people in Weirton I socialized with were Larry's relatives. I became really close with Larry's aunt, who they called Tot. She was an elderly lady originally from the South.

When she reminisced, she reminded me of my younger days, referring to working, soul food, hard times, and many other things that hit home. I often visited her just to chew the fat, as they say. I also helped her in her garden—my forte—and other chores around the house. When she passed away, it hurt me just as if she were my mother. There also was Hugh, Larry's uncle, who was also like a brother to me. When I was about ten years old, Hugh's future wife, Tootie, would come by our house in Rayland to visit with her dad—her dad and my dad both worked in the coal mine. I was in love with that pretty lady.

Since I'm a workaholic, I helped build a deck for Hugh; helped

Larry's mother, Lucy; helped a couple of my neighbors build their decks; and of course, helped Larry. I stayed with Larry at his home for about eight months while building my house. To show my appreciation, I had the bedroom and bathroom that I used painted. I also finished his basement, doing all the carpenter work, the wiring, and plumbing.

In 2013 I sold off all the legal-sized timber on the property, which was one of the fruits of the property. Not long after that, two gentlemen were at my gate. I let them in, and it was a sweet surprise, another fruit of the property. They were from a large oil company and offered me a tidy amount of money for the mineral rights. They said they'd never drill on my property because of being too close to the housing area; instead, they planned to frack. While fracking, they might cross under your property even if they were miles away. It was a deal I couldn't refuse. I couldn't believe that Sam Cusic didn't think to reserve the mineral rights in the deed. But at that time, who knew? I took the money and ran.

MISERY

In 2014 I started having excruciating hip and groin pain. I went to several local orthopedic doctors, and they all said that they couldn't find anything wrong with my hip. But one Pittsburgh doctor who worked in Steubenville Hospital and Allegheny Hospital found that I needed back surgery—again. The side effect of being a workaholic. He didn't want to perform back surgery until the other surgeons identified why I was still experiencing hip and groin pain. He referred me to a coworker who was supposed to be one of the best surgeons in Pennsylvania.

That doctor told me I needed a new hip practically before I walked in the door. I had the surgery immediately, and anyone who's had a total hip replacement knows how much pain and hell you go through. Even though I still had constant hip/groin pain months after hip surgery, I had back surgery. So I had post-surgery back pain on top of post-replacement surgery pain along with the groin pain. I must have gone to the surgeon that performed the hip replacement eight times complaining about the same hip pain. He took several ex-rays and tested for infections but no luck. Mind you, I was taking Percocet, which wasn't helping very much. He finally got frustrated.

"I give up. I'm referring you to a colleague of mine; maybe he can help you."

I went to his colleague three times before he told me, "I'm no expert on hernias, but by the way you're describing your groin pain, I believe you have a hernia. I'm sending you to one of the best hernia doctors in the area."

So off I went to the hernia specialist, who looked at some of my X-rays and said, "Holy shit, I can't believe no one caught this. You have a hernia."

I asked, "Do you mean that I didn't need a hip replacement in the first place?"

"I am not saying that."

I bet he got on the phone immediately after I left his office telling someone they had screwed up.

The hernia was corrected a week later. Now, I have post-surgery pain from the hernia, added to pain from the back and hip surgeries. I was a total mess. I saw ads for the Cleveland Clinic on TV, so I picked an orthopedic doctor out of my hat and called. I got an appointment within a week. I was eating Percocet like its candy, so I needed a driver.

I took the records from all the recent tests and surgeries with me to an infectious disease specialist. She lay me on a table and stuck a seemingly foot-long needle in my hip between the socket and ball of the prosthesis. She wasn't trying to take liquid like all of the other doctors; she was injecting saline. She had me lay there for a few minutes, then drew the saline back out and sent me home, saying she'd get the results back in a couple of days.

Two days later she called me. "Get to this hospital today as soon as possible. You need surgery right away. You have a dry infection hiding in the prosthesis, and if it escapes, you can die."

I couldn't get there quickly enough. It was a three-hour trip driving just over the speed limit. When I made it to the hospital, they took me immediately to surgery. When I woke up, there was a doctor standing over me, apologizing. I asked him why, and he said that he worked on me for nearly two hours trying to remove the prosthesis because it was so well healed.

"I had to break your leg to get the infected prosthesis out."

The X-rays showed a square notch of bone missing at the rim of the femur where the prosthesis shaft would fit into. I can't even begin to tell you how much pain I was in after I was moved from recovery into my room.

I spent sixty days in the hospital, had fourteen blood transfusions, suffered kidney failure, anemia, and low blood pressure. I had tubes sticking out of me everywhere. I didn't tell anyone I was going to the hospital because I didn't want people going out of their way for me. And Cleveland Clinic was quite a hike. But it did leak out after a month because people thought I was dead up on the hill or something. I was in so much pain that I prayed to die more than once. And the bed was too short.

After two months of pain and seemingly torture, I was sent home. Believe it or not, they had a simulator SUV for me to practice getting in and out of. They had to know exactly how I would enter the house and how many steps there were. They had me practice that too.

I was home with no hip for two months. A nurse came every day for an hour the first two weeks and eventually every three days. I had a physical therapist come every day for a month and eventually every three days. I did not want any company. The nurse would warm up a can of soup sometimes. I looked like a skeleton.

Thank God for my friend Huss. I met him a year before I had my surgery saga. He was a car aficionado who collects cars, buys, sells, and restores cars. I met him when I needed a small fuse for my Rolls Royce. He had the exact same year and model. He also had the fuse I needed. We hit it off really fast, and I was amazed at his collection. Huss and his wife chauffeured me up and down that road to Cleveland Clinic countless times, visited me at the hospital, ran errands for me, and brought me dinner countless times. I owe him big time. They saved my life.

I was so bored, and being the workaholic I am, I needed to do *something*, but I didn't know what. With no hip and a walker, I went to the barn about fifty yards away. It had a gravel floor that caused my walker wheels to jam, and down I went. I was lucky that I had my cell phone. I called Larry, and he seemed to get to me in a nanosecond. He cursed me out and got me back to the house.

I went back to Cleveland Clinic for the third surgery on the same hip, opening up the same scar. They did the surgery on Christmas Eve 2015. The surgeon had to insert wire and screws to hold the prosthesis in the femur since there was a piece of bone missing.

Three weeks later I was discharged, and Larry brought me home. I went through the nurse and physical therapy routine again. After being home for about a month, I was lying in bed thinking I was a damn junky. I had my life to live, and I wanted to spend some of my money but not on drugs. I decided to quit taking all meds and stopped cold turkey.

I never thought it could be possible to hurt that badly all over every inch of my body.

When my nurse came, I was a total wreck. She wanted to call 911, but I said no and told her to call Larry. He rushed me to the emergency room. My general practitioner came and explained that I had to come off the drugs gradually. He gave me the formula, and I went home. I did what he told me, and after two days, I said the hell with this and threw the pills away. I was still in a lot of pain, but it wasn't anywhere near the pain that I went through before—and still isn't. After I had a good talk with myself, thanking God for sparing me. Again. I decided to sell almost all my toys—my Harley, my pickup truck, my Camaro convertible, my Rolls Royce, and the Maserati.

I remember going back to the hospital for another post-surgery visit in 2017. Larry was with me, and the doctor floored both of us. He had taken X-rays and expressed surprise because the bone had grown back around the prosthesis so well. He found it hard to believe for a man my age.

I said, "Doc, do you think that I'll be able to golf again."

"Man, you've been through hell, and I doubt it. I don't want to blow smoke up your ass; you're going to be fucked up the rest of your life."

My surgeon was young, cool, and cocky. We couldn't believe our ears, and all we could do was laugh. Never tell me what I can't do. I golfed after that, still did heavy work, and rode my horse. Don't get me wrong, I still hurt today and may have a little gimp at times. I may take Tylenol from time to time and nothing more. I never smoked, never drank beer, was not a whiskey drinker. I do collect wine as a hobby and drink a glass occasionally for dinner and give it as gifts. I weigh the same as I did in college and work out for an hour, five days a week. I am chronologically challenged, but I still feel young at heart. Even so, I try not to let my mind make appointments that my body can't keep.

MEETING SOMEONE VERY SPECIAL AND ANOTHER MOVE

In 2018 I felt like I wasn't going to die anytime soon (but you never know). I went out and bought myself a new Jaguar F-Type convertible, a new Jaguar XE for my everyday car, and a Porsche Cayenne for my truck.

I met a lady in Pittsburgh in a restaurant. She had dropped an earring; I picked it up and asked if it was hers. She said yes. At first I thought she dropped it on purpose, like an eighteenth-century lady from a family of means would do to get the attention of a gentleman of means.

It sounds lame, but I asked her if she was Costa Rican because I detected a Spanish-like accent in her speech. She said she was Brazilian. We were standing in the hallway talking, and I asked if she was with someone. She said she'd left her girlfriend sitting at the bar and invited me to join them if I wished. I did.

We talked for a long time. I learned she was a manager at the Wyndham Hotel. She had previously worked in Orlando at a Wyndham and still had a condominium in Kissimmee. What a coincidence; I had been thinking about selling my house and moving to either Florida or Arizona. I thought: *She just might be the catalyst to move.* One can always dream.

When they were ready to make their exit, I got up the nerve to ask for her phone number. She hesitated then gave it to me. We talked on the phone a few times before asking her out. Our first date was at a restaurant, the second date was horseback riding, and the third an afternoon winery visit. We hit it off pretty fast after we went to each other's houses several times for dinner. Before you knew it, she was moving in with me, and I put my house up for sale because we were heading for Florida. The house was on the market for about a year before a tech guy from the Pittsburgh area who was living in Iran for work saw my house on Zillow and liked it right off.

He made a trip to the States just to view the house and arrived with an expert to assist in inspecting the house. He figured that what he would pay for a house like mine in size and amenities and taxes in Pennsylvania would be ridiculously high. We haggled a few days, and we finally came to an agreement. I would almost get my asking price, and he would get a much larger house with lower taxes only twenty minutes from Pittsburgh. My girlfriend and I made a few trips to Florida before the closing to find a place to live. We found a house half the size of my West Virginia home. I really didn't need a large house again because I never used more than four rooms in the other houses anyway. Let's just say that my last two houses were lucrative flips. I closed on my house in West Virginia and closed on the Florida house the day after.

My girlfriend found a job in Florida at booking.com and resigned from the Wyndham group. Being the workaholic that I am, I was tearing walls out the day after the new house closed. In order to get a flavor of what I had in West Virginia, I put a built-in two-hundred bottle wine refrigerator in the dining room, a stone and granite outdoor kitchen with stainless steel cabinets and drawers, a built-in barbecue grill, microwave, sink with hot and cold water, and a fire pit. A solar power system was installed, a home theatre, a library, and every floor in the house was changed to wood except in the kitchen and the bathrooms.

NEVER GIVE UP

I have purchased or built four new homes in my lifetime, with two of those houses selling for seven figures. All of those houses were in the suburbs, and I've never brought down property values. If anything, I raised property values. I admittedly have a complex. I have to rise above what many White people expect from Black people. I have sometimes gone to an upscale restaurant requiring a suit and tie while many White people were wearing jeans and T-shirts.

From the time I was young well into adulthood, I thought it was just me who felt intimidated by walking into a White establishment. Over the years I have polled Black people from all walks of life about this, and 99 percent of us feel that same way—it's not that we are afraid; it's exhausting dealing with systematic racism throughout life.

I've had some White friends say: "You're exaggerating." In other words, it's my fault that I feel that way. My rebuttal to them is: *Do you ever feel intimated when you walk into a White establishment?* They usually laugh and say no. After explaining what my grandparents, parents, and I have gone through and I still experience, most get it!

I could never bring myself to be below the norm. I have always met the norm and went above and beyond the norm due to no fault of my own. When the days came that I was able to wear designer suits to work every day and not wearing the same suit for two weeks, I felt guilty.

I also felt guilty driving high-end automobiles. I could purchase cars without leaving my house; they delivered them to me in a closed trailer and picked them up when servicing was due, leaving me a loaner car. A maid comes once a week to tidy up, and the lawn service comes to cut my grass once a week. This has been happening for quite a few years, and I love it, but there's still a little guilt. At the same time, that little voice in my head says I deserve it. I think the voice is winning.

When I lived in New Jersey while being a principal, I would stop at a deli that was en route to work almost every morning for a pastry and orange juice. There was a homeless guy sitting outside who knew me by name because I would give him two dollars each time I saw him—sometimes five dollars. The man was disheveled, unshaven, and riddled with tobacco stains. The last time I gave him money, he thought that he would pay me a compliment.

"Some of you people are almost as good as we are."

Wow. There I was dressed in a designer suit and driving a Porsche. That goes to show you that no matter what you have achieved, what your status is, you are still that Black person in the eyes of many. My good friend who tried to co-sign for his grandson's $15,000 loan is a living example.

It's now the year 2021, and I'm not getting any younger, but I'm still that workaholic. I'm presently in the middle of purchasing a parcel of lakefront property located in Lake Lanier, located in Metropolitan Atlanta, where I will personally build/subcontract my vacation getaway home. This will be my bucket list fulfillment and retirement for sure.

I haven't forgotten where I came from because six of my siblings, my children, granddaughter, and great-granddaughter all receive a monetary gift for Christmas and birthdays. In the near future, I will have a revocable trust fund. I will give my children monthly monetary gifts while I am still alive! All my dad left us was a funeral bill. Why not give a boost to my children now so they can enjoy it instead of waiting until I croak? Besides, by then they might be too old to enjoy it.

During the trauma with my hip surgery, a nurse held my hand and said that all the suffering and near-deaths means something—that God had a plan for me. That would be about the third time I heard that in my lifetime.

Since I started writing this book, Trump lost the 2020 presidential election, and he incited an insurrection at the US Capitol by White supremacists, Nazis, QAnon conspiracy theorists, and thousands of other White people of all walks of life. I've witnessed Black men and women being shot or murdered by bad policemen causing BLM demonstrations all over the world. Republicans are pushing gerrymandering and passing state laws to restrict voting rights for people of color in an effort to retain power at any cost. I witnessed much the same thing growing up with Jim Crow laws in the South. Now it's Jim Crow on steroids—déjà vu.

With all of that being said, I am still optimistic about things getting better. I have been to dozens of other countries, but there is no country like the United States. Regardless of the inequalities, I—and many more people of color—were able to achieve individual success. That gives me hope that no matter what creed or color, people will be able to be successful on an even keel. I don't believe that I nor my children and granddaughter will live to see that even keel happen. We can always hope that my great-granddaughter will live to witness an even keel.

Thank God for Martin Luther King, those that were with him, those who took up the mantel and are still carrying it, and those people who aren't afraid to live up to their White privilege. What a wonderful world it would be if all people would open up their minds and hearts.

As the late great John Lewis would say: Never give up! Keep your eyes on the prize!

CPSIA information can be obtained
at www.ICGtesting.com
Printed in the USA
BVHW030812151121
621189BV00032B/671/J